Keats as a Narrative Poet

Keats
as a
Narrative Poet
A Test of Invention

Judy Little

UNIVERSITY OF NEBRASKA PRESS · LINCOLN

Publishers on the Plains

UNP

*The publication of this book was assisted by a grant from
The Andrew W. Mellon Foundation.*

Library of Congress Cataloging in Publication Data

Little, Judy, 1941–
  Keats as a narrative poet.

  Bibliography: p.
  Includes index.
  1. Keats, John, 1795–1821—Criticism and interpreta-
tion. I. Title.
PR4837.L56   821'.7   74–81365
ISBN 0–8032–0846–4

To Bernice Slote

Contents

I

Introduction

The revolutionary impulse which demands new values and new
literary forms does not always present the poet with an instanta-
neously complete world view, and with literary architectures
which can embody the new values. The "new" is by definition
untried, tentative, exploratory. Although the romantic movement in literature is still difficult to define precisely, the romantics themselves were certain of one characteristic of their time:
they felt that it was radically new and that history and literature
were being nudged into new directions. Wordsworth's well-
known description of his response to the initial stages of the
French Revolution expresses his excitement at living near the
beginning of a new age:

> Bliss was it in that dawn to be alive,
> But to be young was very Heaven![1]

The events on the Continent represented a dawn; history was
starting afresh. Wordsworth, along with Blake and Shelley, attempted long poetic statements which were at least in part a
response to this strong sense of historical change. John Keats,
while not as politically conscious as some of the romantics, nevertheless participated in the literary revolution, experimenting
with new narrative structures in his persistent attempt to write
a long, great work. Unlike his later critics, who usually value the
odes and his highly polished sensuous imagery, Keats measured
himself against his great ambition, the ambition of writing a

monumental poem. Even though he recognized that his first long work, *Endymion,* was uncertain and immature and even though he did not complete his epic on the subject of Hyperion, his continuing experimentation with longer forms resulted in narrative verse which effectively solved the most important structural problems facing poets early in the nineteenth century. Narrative poetry was to some extent a hazardous undertaking for a poet at this time, because history as well as literature was in a state of experimentation. A brief look at the consequences of this experimentation, and a review of Keats's attitude toward the long poem, will be useful before turning to his narrative works.

Although literary periods have very blurred edges, historians and literary scholars agree that in the eighteenth century a fairly coherent world view prevailed and that the French Revolution, beginning in 1789, is an event which can conveniently mark the deterioration of this world view. Earl Wasserman enumerates some of the basic attitudes characteristic of the era just before the hypothetical boundaries of the romantic period began:

> In varying degrees, ranging from conviction to faith and to passive submission, man accepted, to name but a few, the Christian interpretation of history, the sacramentalism of nature, the Great Chain of Being, the analogy of the various planes of creation, the conception of man as microcosm, and, in the literary area, the doctrine of the genres.[2]

The ideas mentioned here were already old in the eighteenth century; they had been growing roots for hundreds of years and could serve as the sustaining landscape for literature. According to the historian John Randall, however, after the collapse of this eighteenth-century world view, the main directions of history have become increasingly difficult to describe; the nineteenth and the twentieth centuries may be part of a continuing period of transition toward some future synthesis of a new world view.[3] Whatever happened at the eighteenth-century turning point seems to be still happening. The diverse meanings which the word *romanticism* has accumulated, and the continuing efforts to define the assumptions of this movement, may testify to the fact that the "movement" is not yet finished. Arthur Lovejoy regards the confusion in the use of the term *romanticism* as "the scandal of literary history and criticism." [4] If the world is still moving toward some redefinition, some new synthesis of values with which to replace that lost in the eighteenth century, then we are still in the "romantic movement," and hence too close to it to perceive adequately its outlines. The romantic writers themselves were even closer than we are to the confused beginnings of the new era; to the extent that narrative poetry, particularly the epic, depends on perspective, on myth, and on the accumulation of a cultural tradition, these poets were at a disadvantage. The epics of Virgil and Milton were written at the culmination, the end of the tradition which each poem represents, not at its cloudy and uncertain beginnings.

Successful narrative poetry does not entirely depend on a definable world view, however, nor did history and literature suddenly become utterly amorphous after 1789. Certain characteristics developed prominence, and some of these help to illuminate more sharply the problems which Keats, and the poets who shared his ambition of composing long works, had to confront and resolve. For instance, literary scholars often point to the increasingly subjective quality of poetry written in the last two hundred years. Although long poems traditionally had a sustaining structure of objective, external event, the romantic poets attempted long subjective structures, Wordsworth by means of slow-moving blank verse conversations in *The Excursion,* for example, and Blake by means of an elaborate and personal visionary world. It is just this inward turning which proved to be, in the view of some critics, a disaster for any extended poetic work.

In his essay, "The Long Poem in the Age of Wordsworth," A. C. Bradley suggests that a reader's disappointment in the long poems of this period is largely the result of their "inward or subjective tendency." [5] But the romantics, writing at the beginning of an era, could not always appropriately work within older conventions. As D. G. James has observed, these poets were "necessarily innovators." [6] And they frequently attempted with their innovations the most abstruse nondramatic subjects, trying to image the deep truth and offering fragmen-

3

tary glimpses of ultimate reality. The cost of this visionary inward turning was the loss of what would ordinarily be considered subject matter; as Harold Bloom remarks: "Wordsworth's Copernican revolution in poetry is marked by the evanescence of any subject but subjectivity, the loss of what a poem is 'about.' " [7] The immediate challenge for the romantics was to experiment with new literary architectures which could give some kind of shape to the new psychological orientation.

The romantic poets did not turn their backs completely on traditional genres, nor did they abandon the Western world's inheritance of myth. They did, however, widen the boundaries of conventional patterns, and they altered and expanded some of the myths. As M. H. Abrams expresses it, the romantic poets tend to "lyricize" the longer forms, substituting the qualities of lyric poetry for plot, character, and action.[8] More specifically, Karl Kroeber observes that a poet who writes romantic narration usually rearranges his subject matter and places the emphasis on lyric qualities, pictorial beauty, timelessness, and the stylization of character. Kroeber designates as "discontinuous structure" the free utilization of narrative elements within a lyric or a visionary poem; because of his essentially lyric orientation, the romantic writer usually abandons a straightforward sequential narrative for the discontinuous structure which "is demanded by the poet's efforts to express that which is not objective." [9] Keats's *Endymion* demonstrates some of the hazards of "discontinuous structure"; the narrative, the on-going action, of this poem is sometimes nearly lost in the apparent miscellany of the hero's visions and the elaborately described caves and bowers which delay his progress. *Endymion* illustrates also the romantic habit of greatly extending and altering the implications of classic myths. Keats recognized that the tale of a love affair between the moon and a man was only "one bare circumstance," and he set himself the task of expanding this circumstance into a romance of four thousand lines.[10] After the expansion, Endymion seems to represent man or the poet, or some impulse within the human mind; the character is symbolic, and his search for Cynthia evidently represents a search for beauty or truth or a full maturation of the imaginative powers. Another example of the romantic poet's alteration of myth is Shelley's *Prometheus Unbound.* When Shelley uses the Prometheus myth it is no longer a drama concerning man's relationship with the gods; it is more like an extended lyric poem with dialogue, and it evidently describes a pattern of salvation which may be psychological, social, metaphysical, or all three. Wasserman, for instance, in his very coherent and detailed analysis of the poem, argues that Prometheus represents ultimate reality, the "One Mind." [11] Such ontological subject matter is not entirely incompatible with the dramatic mode, but unusual imaginative resources are required in order to portray it under the dramatic guise of several characters, time, and suspense.

The problems and dangers involved in moving poetic structures away from the objective and the dramatic did not have to await the special discovery of modern critics. Keats himself recognized the ineffectiveness, for poetry, of too much subjectivity; he suggested that the "poetical Character" is to be "distinguished from the wordsworthian or egotistical sublime." The poet should have no "self"; instead he takes "as much delight in conceiving an Iago as an Imogen. What shocks the virtuous philosopher, delights the camelion Poet." [12] Keats, in these remarks, is identifying a problem that has persisted into the twentieth century and which has now been recognized as a problem of fiction as well as poetry. Virginia Woolf, for instance, experimenting with nontraditional prose structures rather than verse narratives, recognized that her inward looking novels must try to avoid the limited perspective of the "damned egotistical self." [13] A writer may of course choose to let his own personality be the chief thing that calls attention to his work and which gives it the semblance of structural unity. A recent critic has remarked of Byron that "it is Byron, and Byron's idea of himself, which holds his work together." [14] But Keats did not respect Byron's ability to project his own strong ego; according to Keats, Byron merely "cuts a figure." [15] Keats did not want to cut a figure; that is, he did not want to become a symbol for his work.

In order to avoid the subjectivity of mere egotism while at the same time avoiding also the literary and cultural formulations which were inappropriate to a new age, the romantic poet had to create a world as well as a poem. Wasserman precisely defines this challenge: "By the end of the eighteenth century —and ever since—the poet has been required to conceive his own structure of order, his own more-than-linguistic syntax, and so to engage that structure that the poetic act is creative both of a cosmic system and of the poem made possible by that system." [16] The poet, in the last two hundred years, has had an added responsibility; his verbal structure must create the context, the world view, the complex of values, in which the poem is to be understood. This task of embodying a "cosmic system" in the structural network of a poem is a very large task indeed. It is not one which the romantic poets shirked, but neither is it a responsibility which they fulfilled with entire success. The conflicting critical interpretations, for instance, of the structure and significance of Endymion's quest, suggest that the values and the world view of the poem are insufficiently incorporated into the narrative statement. The ambiguities of this work, however, may be at least partly the result of the romantic cultural milieu. The profuse complexities of Blake—who certainly attempted to create a world—and the meditatively exploratory blank verse of Wordsworth's long poems, may owe much to the exuberant flexibilities of a consciously "new" era.

The very attempt to build symbolic structures in such an era, whether these structures entirely succeed or not, reveals a great deal about a poet's energy and imagination. A long poem, especially, allows the reader to watch a poet synthesize a world; in an extended work the poet can submit an idea, or a "circumstance," to use Keats's word, to a series of climactic evaluations, or develop its implications along an involved linear structure. If a writer does not use the traditional devices of action, character development, climax, and resolution, he will have to accomplish by means of some new formal patterns the sense of sustained impact which only a long work can give. The poet who is consciously writing in a new age will probably find that the formal challenge presents an especially exciting test of his creative imagination.

Keats readily accepted the opportunities for such a test. As he worked on *Endymion,* he wrote: "It will be a test, a trial of my Powers of Imagination and chiefly of my invention which is a rare thing indeed"; *Endymion* was to be a test of his stature as a poet, for he went on to ask in the same letter: "Did our great Poets ever write short Pieces?" [17] Keats implies here that a great poet is by definition one who writes a long work. His own efforts to live up to this definition, and the innovative structural patterns of his narrative poems, have been generally over-looked by critics. The narrative poems which he completed—*Endymion, Isabella, The Eve of St. Agnes, La Belle Dame sans Merci,* and *Lamia*—demonstrate a sensitivity to structure which is fully as intelligent as his ability to handle the lyrical and descriptive elements of his shorter works. Even the fragments, *Hyperion* and *The Fall of Hyperion,* show a perceptive, experi-mental concept of epic poetry.

Keats's ambition to write an epic probably began when he read and translated the *Aeneid* while at school. His remarks about this classical epic suggest an attentive observation of the formal elements of such a poem. He astonished his friend Charles Cowden Clarke, whose father directed the school, by remarking that "there was feebleness in the structure of the work." After leaving the school in 1811 to study surgery, Keats frequently visited Clarke, and now impressed his friend most by his responses to the smaller poetic elements: the imagery and striking epithets of the *Faerie Queene*.[18] And, once Keats became interested in Leigh Hunt's theories about improving the heroic couplet, his earlier concern for the total work appar-ently narrowed temporarily to a pleasure in verbal minutiae; his fellow medical student Henry Stephens notes that Keats "was fond of Imagery, The most trifling Similes appeared to please him." [19] This remark suggests that Keats's acquaintance with Hunt may have diverted his interests away from the larger formal relationships necessary to hold a long work together.[20] And yet his one great aim persisted. In his own mind at least, all of Keats's endeavors in poetry were, as H. W. Garrod has observed, "subsidiary only, and preliminary, to 'the long poem.'" [21] Even when he was ill at Rome during the last months of his life, his companion Joseph Severn records that he often spoke of a projected "long Poem on the story of Sabrina as left by Milton." [22]

There have been some attempts to explain this obsession. Perhaps his friend Haydon, the painter, encouraged Keats to try something on the heroic scale.[23] Also, Keats read and enjoyed several extremely long poems, some of them of major literary worth, others of dubious value. He read Virgil's *Aeneid,* Dante's *Commedia,* and Tasso's *Jerusalem Delivered;* he read *Paradise Lost* several times. Perhaps his interest in lengthy works was partly inspired by Elizabethan models; he took the motto for the verse epistles of the 1817 volume from a rambling episodic Elizabethan poem, *Brittania's Pastorals,* and his friend Charles Brown asserts that Keats's genius was first awakened by Spenser's *Faerie Queene.*[24] In addition to long Renaissance works, Keats read Beattie's eighteenth-century poem *The Minstrel* and Mary Tighe's *Psyche,* first published in 1805; in 1818 he writes of his former delight in these poets.[25] He also thought Wordsworth's poem *The Excursion* was, along with Haydon's paintings and Hazlitt's taste, one of the three things to rejoice at in the age.[26] He evidently rejoiced in all of these lengthy poems, and his admiration for epic poetry he may have inherited from the eighteenth century. During this period, as Raymond D. Havens has thoroughly documented, the popularity of *Paradise Lost* was overwhelming, and it was widely imitated; between 1705 and 1800 there were over one hundred editions of *Paradise Lost,* while Shakespeare's plays went through only fifty editions.[27] Keats might have noticed in *The Excursion* that the Wanderer's literary preferences were in agreement with the eighteenth-century admiration of Milton. In his youth, the Wanderer spent "what small overplus / His earnings might supply" on

> The book that most had tempted his desires
> While at the stall he read. Among the hills
> He gazed upon that mighty orb of song,
> The divine Milton.[28]

All of England agreed with the Wanderer's opinion of Milton; it is no wonder that Keats shared the general admiration for the nation's foremost epic poet.

Keats gives credit to Clarke for having shown him the primacy of the epic:

> Shew'd me that epic was of all the king,
> Round, vast, and spanning all like Saturn's ring.[29]

Introduction

If an epic is to be "Round, vast, and spanning all," and if it is to be written at the beginning of a new age, then it will have to create within itself the world view which it spans, the context of myth and assumptions by which it is to be understood; the poet will have to create a cosmic system, as Wasserman affirms, as well as a poem. Keats did not complete his single epic, but his ambition to write such a work did much to redesign narrative verse, giving it forms more appropriate to the inward and lyrical orientation of much romantic poetry.

Keats may have felt that some of his shorter narratives were not quite worthy of his highest ambitions. He refers to *The Eve of St. Mark* as "little," and he places *Lamia* in the same category as the "two Tales" of *Isabella* and *The Eve of St. Agnes.*[30] Nevertheless, these poems, with the exception of *The Eve of St. Mark,* do develop an extended narrative and do present the poet with structural opportunities and difficulties similar to those of his larger poetic endeavors, *Endymion* and the fragments of his epic *(Hyperion* and *The Fall of Hyperion).* Even the very short ballad, *La Belle Dame sans Merci,* shows Keats confronting and successfully resolving the narrative problems of construction and characterization, problems of continuing importance to his great ambition.

In addition to his recognizably "narrative" works, some of the longer poems in the 1817 volume proved to be very productive experiments. Walter Jackson Bate calls the verse epistles examples of "longer, non-lyric forms" to which Keats was attracted because of his desire to write a long poem.[31] The verse epistles are in fact quite important in an examination of the structure of Keats's narrative poems, for in these epistles he experiments with a pattern of repetition which, I believe, is the shaping framework of *Endymion.* The early verse letters are therefore included in this study.

Some of Keats's longer poems, or fragments of projected poems, cannot very appropriately be discussed. The fragment "Calidore," for instance, is too slight for analysis. The more interesting fragment "The Cap and Bells" manifests little structural artistry, although considerable artistry in other respects. The dramas, *Otho the Great* and *King Stephen,* are omitted here, since his collaborator, Charles Brown, rather than Keats himself, was responsible for the plot of *Otho the Great; King Stephen* is too small a fragment to bear examination.

The poems themselves are given most attention in this study, but some consideration of literary "theory" often clarifies what Keats means and what he produces. Although a comprehensive statement of the poetic theory of Hunt, Hazlitt, or Keats, would not be relevant here, the critical concepts which had structural implications for Keats require examination; these concepts helped him to refine and develop his persistent hope of embodying in the narrative poetry of a new age his ambition to be a great poet. Recent criticism has already sufficiently established the long-obscured fact that Keats could think as well as write, and there is growing critical testimony that both of these abilities went into his work, and especially into the great odes. It is the larger structures whose intelligence I wish to demonstrate; most of these show the innovative virtuosity which we might expect in a poet whose sensitive control of the smaller elements in his work has long been recognized.

Notes

1. William Wordsworth, *The Prelude, or Growth of a Poet's Mind,* ed. Ernest de Selincourt, 2d ed., rev. Helen Darbishire (Oxford: Clarendon Press, 1959), bk. 11, lines 108–9.

2. Earl Wasserman, *The Subtler Language* (Baltimore: Johns Hopkins Press, 1959), pp. 10–11.

3. John Herman Randall, Jr., *The Making of the Modern Mind,* rev. ed. (Boston: Houghton Mifflin Co., 1968), pp. 389–91.

4. Arthur O. Lovejoy, *Essays in the History of Ideas* (Baltimore: Johns Hopkins Press, 1948), p. 234.

5. A. C. Bradley, "The Long Poem in the Age of Wordsworth," in *Oxford Lectures on Poetry* (London: Macmillan & Co., 1926), p. 187.

6. D. G. James, *The Romantic Comedy* (London: Oxford University Press, 1948), p. 124.

7. Harold Bloom, "The Internalization of Quest Romance," *Yale Review* 58 (1969): 528. For further discussion of romantic subjectivity, see James, *Romantic Comedy,* pp. 80–81, and D. R. Rauber, "The Fragment as Romantic Form," *Modern Language Quarterly* 30 (June 1969): 212–21.

8. M. H. Abrams, *The Mirror and the Lamp* (New York: Oxford University Press, 1953), p. 98.

9. Karl Kroeber, *Romantic Narrative Art* (Madison: University of Wisconsin Press, 1960), pp. 66, 51–58.

10. *The Letters of John Keats,* ed. Hyder Edward Rollins, 2 vols. (Cambridge, Mass.: Harvard University Press, 1958), 1:170.

11. Earl Wasserman, *Shelley's Prometheus Unbound* (Baltimore: Johns Hopkins Press, 1965), pp. 1–38.

12. *Letters of John Keats,* 1:386–87.

13. Virginia Woolf, *A Writer's Diary,* ed. Leonard Woolf (London: The Hogarth Press, 1954), p. 23.

14. Paul West, ed., *Byron: A Collection of Critical Essays* (Englewood Cliffs, N.J.: Prentice-Hall, 1963), p. 2.

15. *Letters of John Keats,* 2:67.

16. Wasserman, *Subtler Language,* p. 172.

17. *Letters of John Keats,* 1:169–70.

18. Charles and Mary Cowden Clarke, *Recollections of Writers* (New York: Charles Scribner's Sons, 1878), pp. 124, 126. Clarke makes a similar statement about Keats's "delight" in the imagery and the epithets of Spenser in notes sent to Richard Monckton Milnes; see *The Keats Circle,* ed. Hyder Edward Rollins, 2 vols. (Cambridge, Mass.: Harvard University Press, 1948), 2:149.

19. *Keats Circle,* 2:209.

20. Keats continued to be attentive to the smaller structures of poetry—to the really stylistic elements. He remarks in August 1819: "I look upon fine Phrases like a Lover"; see *Letters of John Keats,* 2:139.

21. H. W. Garrod, *Keats,* 2d ed. (Oxford: Clarendon Press, 1939), p. 64.

22. *Keats Circle,* 2:138.

23. E. C. Pettet, *On the Poetry of Keats* (London: Cambridge University Press, 1957), pp. 14–15.

24. Joan Grundy, "Keats and the Elizabethans," in *John Keats: A Reassessment,* ed. Kenneth Muir (Liverpool: Liverpool University Press, 1959), pp. 5–9; for Brown's remark, see *Keats Circle,* 2:55.

25. *Letters of John Keats,* 2:18; for further discussion of Keats and Tighe, see Earle V. Weller, ed., *Keats and Mary Tighe* (New York: Century Co., for The Modern Language Association of America, 1928), pp. vii–xvi.

26. *Letters of John Keats,* 1:203.

27. Raymond D. Havens, *The Influence of Milton on English Poetry* (Cambridge, Mass.: Harvard University Press, 1922), pp. 4–5.

28. William Wordsworth, *The Excursion,* bk. 1, lines 244–50, in *The Poetical Works of William Wordsworth,* ed. Ernest de Selincourt and Helen Darbishire, 5 vols. (Oxford: Clarendon Press, 1940–49), 5:16. All further quotations from the poetry of Wordsworth are from this edition and indicated by line number in the text.

29. "To Charles Cowden Clarke," lines 66–67, in *The Poetical Works,* ed. H. W. Garrod, 2d ed. (London: Oxford University Press, 1958). All further quotations from the poetry of Keats are from this edition and indicated by line number in the text.

30. See his references to "a little Poem call'd 'St. Agnes Eve'" (*Letters of John Keats,* 2:58), "a little thing call'd the 'eve of St. Mark'"

(ibid., p. 62), and his remark: "I have written two Tales, one from Boccacio call'd the Pot of Basil; and another call'd St. Agnes' Eve on a popular superstition; and a third call'd Lamia—" (ibid., p. 139).

31. Walter Jackson Bate, *John Keats* (Cambridge, Mass.: Harvard University Press, Belknap Press, 1963), p. 76.

II

Experimentation: The 1817 Volume

Keats published his first book of poems in 1817, and in this volume he was already pursuing his goal of writing a long work. Although few of these poems, except some of the sonnets, move securely and directly from beginning to end, even those that are fragments testify to the large impulse that made Keats persist in his effort to give momentum to a narrative. It is not surprising that Keats has trouble prodding a poem beyond its first line; his friend Leigh Hunt's almost exclusive focus on achieving "variety" in the couplet not only led Keats to adopt a limp line, but diverted and perhaps hindered the poet's search for effective ways of arranging good lines into the larger structure of a good poem. Nevertheless, some of the poems of Keats's first volume, especially "I Stood Tip-Toe upon a Little Hill" and the verse epistles, do show deliberate if sometimes artificial experimentation with structures capable of sustaining a large work. In the verse epistle to George Keats and "I Stood Tip-Toe" Keats describes a state of meditative trance in which a poet's imaginative response to the landscape repeats and varies elements of the scene; the structure of parallel imagery which he develops in these two poems he exploits more fully in *Endymion* and in the Hyperion fragments.

Even in the fragments of the 1817 volume, the narrator expresses his hopeful ambition of telling a long story, a chivalric tale. In the "Specimen of an Induction to a Poem," however, he cannot get beyond the necessity to "tell a tale" (1, 11, 45) and into the story itself. "Calidore," another false start, is identified

in the subtitle as "A Fragment." These efforts have been discussed as adequately as such failures may be discussed,[1] and
there is no need to reiterate their shortcomings here. In the
extant lines of these fragments there is no suspense, no expectation set up, no contrast or conflict suggested which could give
the meandering narrative any direction. When he wrote the
poems of this volume, Keats was probably not thinking much
about the direction of the over-all action; he was, under the
influence of Hunt, thinking more about couplets and images
than about the structure of the whole poem.

Since Hunt's ideas about poetry contributed to the difficulties
which Keats experienced as he tried to structure long works, a
brief examination of the literary relationship of the two men
will be useful before looking at the more successful poems in
Keats's first book. Keats became acquainted with Hunt's ideas
before he met the man himself. Through his reading of the
Examiner with Clarke, he had probably accepted the editorial
slant of Hunt in matters of poetry as well as politics; Keats's
reaction to events in France in the years 1814 and 1815 reflect
the views of the older man, and Keats's poem "On Peace"
expresses a hope similar to that held by Hunt in the spring of
1814.[2] In February 1815, Keats wrote a sonnet celebrating
Hunt's release from prison, and by November he had read
Hunt's *The Feast of the Poets*—probably the 1814 or the 1815
edition—where he found Hunt's miscellaneous theories of
prosody in the voluminous notes.[3] There is some uncertainty as
to just when Keats met Hunt in person, although the most likely
date seems to be soon after 9 October 1816.[4]

Hunt's critical vocabulary, as he uses it in *The Feast of the
Poets*, is hardly precise. Nevertheless, some contours of his literary "theory," and some of his preferences among writers, are
apparent. Hunt argues for the "natural" and "simple" in style
and content; he supports, though with some exceptions, Wordsworth's views as expressed in the Preface to *Lyrical Ballads.* As
Claude Lee Finney has observed, however, Hunt wishes to add
to Wordsworth's style the pastoral conventions of Renaissance
writers and the friendly, even cockney sociability of the city.[5]
Along with the "natural" and "simple," Hunt extols "fancy,"
and "variety"; he tends to praise poems, even long ones, for

short passages of ornate "loveliness" rather than to comment on the strength, or weakness, of the over-all structure.

In Hunt's view simplicity and naturalness are well demonstrated by James Thomson's *Castle of Indolence:* "in copying the simplicity together with the quaintnesses of a great poet, he [Thomson] became more natural, and really touched his subject with a more original freshness, than when he had his style to himself." [6] The "natural," then, as Hunt understands it, certainly includes the contributions of allegory. Hunt disagrees with Wordsworth's strictures on personification and "poetic diction"; and he tries to clarify the proper use of metaphor and classical allusion by asserting that either an artificial language or a simple style is suitable as long as one is not mixed with the other, and as long as both refer "to natural emotions." [7]

Along with his advocation of the natural and the simple, Hunt urges that some modifications be made in the heroic couplet. He objects to the metrical artifice of the neoclassic poets, although his own suggestions for repairing the heroic couplet yield a line that is artificial in its own way and at the same time much less effective. He complains that the later followers of Pope have carried the heroic couplet "to its extreme pitch of sameness" and that Pope's versification itself is praised for the very quality it lacks: its "harmony" is, to Hunt's ears, merely a want of "contrast." Some variation is necessary, says Hunt, for "passion and fancy naturally speak a various language." [8] Among other things, the caesura should be varied and should not fall for so many lines consistently on the strong fourth syllable.[9] The best discussion of the details of Hunt's recommendations for improving the heroic couplet (which of course then ceases to be a heroic couplet properly speaking) is given by Bate in *The Stylistic Development of John Keats;* for Hunt's "variety" Bate more accurately substitutes "laxity" and gives ample evidence that Keats surpassed Hunt in this respect, employing even more frequently the devices of "variety": hiatus, run-on lines, feminine rhymes, and the caesura in a weak position, usually in the second half of the line and often following an unstressed syllable.[10] Hunt himself apparently suspected that Keats carried to extremes these suggestions for improving the couplet; in 1844, Hunt observes: "His Endymion, in resolving to be free from all critical trammels, had no versification." [11]

Earlier in the century, however, Hunt was advocating "variety," particularly in a long work such as Spenser's *Faerie Queene;* Hunt objected to Thomas Warton's suggestions for regularizing the "harmony" of a line of this poem.[12] Hunt's attention here is directed to the line, which is of course the basic unit of poetry; he does not offer criticism of the large structural features of this long work. He delights in "the coy loveliness" of Thomas Campbell's *Gertrude of Wyoming,* which he has read several times and which he recommends as the "first" poem of "any length, that has been produced in the present day." [13] Hunt's own fragmentary poem *The Nymphs* (published 1818) demonstrates, by its very thorough lack of formal organization, the necessity of such artifice in a large work; some attention must be given either to the traditional narrative devices of suspense and climax, the dramatic elements of contrast and characterization, or to the deliberate contrivance of some other appropriate organizational features. More than variety and coy loveliness are needed to sustain a long poem.

When Keats expresses admiration for the natural and the simple, he evidently uses these notions in much the same sense as Hunt does. His sonnet on the pseudo-Chaucerian poem *The Flower and the Leaf* suggests that Keats, like Hunt, understands its "white simplicity" to include a very artificial subject matter and treatment ("This Pleasant Tale," 9). *The Flower and the Leaf* abounds in passages of elaborate, detailed description and is rich in allusion and allegorical trappings. In another sonnet, Keats responds to Hunt's poem *The Story of Rimini.* Keats describes this narrative work as a "sweet tale," and a "bower" for the spirit ("On 'The Story of Rimini,' " 3, 12). He is finding here the same thing that Hunt finds in the "coy loveliness" of *Gertrude of Wyoming.* Both Hunt and Keats are, in these remarks, finding about all there is in these poems, of course. The point is that neither Hunt's models nor his theory provided Keats with any distinct idea of how to get from the beginning to the end of a lengthy poem.

Keats was determined, nevertheless, to write a major work; he wanted to test his "invention." In the spring of 1817 he wrote to his brother George that *Endymion* "will be a test, a trial of my Powers of Imagination and chiefly of my invention which is a rare thing indeed—by which I must make 4000 Lines of one bare circumstance and fill them with Poetry." A few sentences later he continues on the same theme: "Besides a long Poem is a test of Invention which I take to be the Polar Star of Poetry, as Fancy is the Sails, and Imagination the Rudder." [14] The ominous thing here is the primacy given to invention, which for Keats, early in his career, suggested the process of amassing incidents sufficient to swell a poem to its desired length.

This emphasis on invention Keats may have derived from earlier writers. Sidney Colvin has suggested that in his "reiterated insistence on Invention and Imagination as the prime endowments of a poet, Keats closely echoes Joseph Warton's protest uttered seventy years before: is this because he had read and remembered it, or only because the same words came naturally to him in pleading the same cause?" [15] Perhaps Keats had read Joseph Warton's praise of Milton's "Nativity Ode" for its "imagination," and of Thomson's *Seasons* for its "copious fancy"; at the same time he would have noticed that Warton's appraisal of Pope's pastorals, for instance, was less glowing, for these lacked new images and "invention." [16] Certainly Keats was acquainted with *The Feast of the Poets,* and Hunt, as we have seen, was acquainted with the work of Joseph's brother, Thomas Warton. The meaning which Keats attaches to *invention* is not far from that of Thomas Warton, who praises Spenser's several descriptions of "bowers" and "gardens" for being each distinct and new, even though they are basically the same situation: "All which, though in general the same, his invention has diversified with many new circumstances." Invention diversifies bowers and gardens with many new circumstances; Keats's first efforts in the narrative poem demonstrate only too well this matter and this method. Later, contrasting Ariosto and Spenser, Warton notes that the Italian poet creates relatively few allegorical beings as compared with Spenser, "for a picturesque invention was by no means his talent." [17] While he attacks Thomas Warton's suggestions for amending Spenser's versification, Hunt's own praise of the fancy and invention of the allegorical *Castle of Indolence* indicates that he and Warton agree basically on the value of this element; Hunt writes of Thomson's poem: "There is more of invention in it,—more of unassisted fancy and abstract enjoyment." [18]

In addition to a knowledge, perhaps via Hunt, of the Wartons' observations on invention, Keats may very well have noticed Addison's remarks in the *Spectator;* Charles Brown notes that this work was in Keats's library. Addison observes that the poet who pursues the "Fairie way of Writing" loses sight of nature; yet the way of fantasy is the most challenging one, for the writer "has no Pattern to follow in it, and must work altogether out of his own Invention." [19] From whatever source Keats derived his understanding of poetic invention, he certainly accepted, in his early poetry, the challenge of the fairy way. His acquaintance with Hunt, and with writers whom Hunt admired, suggests that invention probably implied for Keats at this time a poetic texture of coy loveliness, fantasy, bowers, and gardens. It is remarkable, considering the implications which invention had for him, that his early efforts to write a long poem, and especially *Endymion,* are not more unwieldy chunks of language than they are.

Among these early efforts, the most significant structural experimentations in the 1817 volume are "Sleep and Poetry," "I Stood Tip-Toe," and the three verse epistles. "Sleep and Poetry" is the longest of these, but it is the most uncertain structurally. In "I Stood Tip-Toe" and in the epistles, on the other hand, Keats's experimentation with structure is more successful. The pattern of repeated images, which he uses in "I Stood Tip-Toe," is one that becomes very important in several of his later, longer works.

"Sleep and Poetry" is not a narrative, so one does not expect to find here an action begun and completed with appropriate complication of incident and conflict, or contrast of character. Nevertheless, some relationship of parts to the whole should be distinguishable. If such a relationship exists, it is not very clear, however. One would like to make this poem "work." There is the adumbration of an apparently very important distinction between the poetry of "Flora" (101–2) and that which will record the "agonies, the strife / Of human hearts" (124–25). Maybe the poem is not quite a "scrap-book of Keats's mind at the time," as Amy Lowell says,[20] but it almost is.

Experimentation: The 1817 Volume

The poem begins with a series of tedious questions, all seeking to discover what is more "gentle" and "soothing" than summer, a hummer (a bee), flowers, bowers, dales, nightingales; the answer is that *sleep* is better than all these (1–18). And better than sleep, is *Poesy*, which becomes explicitly the subject of the poem at line 47. The poet sees a mysterious "vision" of a charioteer (Apollo) which apparently represents a glimpse of what the best poetry should be (122–54); next, he attacks what he considers to be the shortcomings of neoclassic poetry (162–206), and then he offers to define the "great end / Of poesy": to "sooth the cares, and lift the thoughts of man" (206–47). The poet expresses doubts about his high ambitions and then finishes the poem with a description of the art objects in the room of Hunt's house where he is spending the night.[21]

Discussions of the formal aspects of this poem generally make use of Wordsworth's "Tintern Abbey" lines and a letter which Keats writes well over a year after composing "Sleep and Poetry"; according to this view, the "three stages" of a poet's life become the main organizational feature of the poem. Since the passage from Keats's letter describing the "apartments" of human life is so important to the interpretation of the poem as representing the "stages" of a poet's development, it must be quoted here:

> I compare human life to a large Mansion of Many Apartments, two of which I can only describe, the doors of the rest being as yet shut upon me—The first we step into we call the infant or thoughtless Chamber, in which we remain as long as we do not think—We remain there a long while, and notwithstanding the doors of the second Chamber remain wide open, showing a bright appearance, we care not to hasten to it; but are at length imperceptibly impelled by the awakening of the thinking principle—within us—we no sooner get into the second Chamber, which I shall call the Chamber of Maiden-Thought, than we become intoxicated with the light and the atmosphere, we see nothing but pleasant wonders, and think of delaying there for ever in delight: However among the effects this breathing is father of is that tremendous one of sharpening one's vision into the heart and nature of Man—of convincing ones nerves that the World is full of Misery and Heartbreak, Pain, Sickness and oppression—whereby This Chamber of Maiden Thought becomes gradually darken'd and at the same time on all sides of it many doors are set open—but all dark—all leading to dark passages—

We see not the ballance of good and evil. We are in a Mist— *We are now in that State*—We feel the "burden of the Mystery," To this point was Wordsworth come, as far as I can conceive when he wrote "Tintern Abbey" and it seems to me that his Genius is explorative of those dark Passages.[22]

If Keats is talking about "stages" of life in "Sleep and Poetry," he certainly does not use the idea for the over-all form of the poem; he drops it at line 162, leaving the rest of the poem a dangling remnant of digression, self-doubt conflicting with re-newed courage, and finally a description of the room where he is spending this night uneasily between sleep and poetry.

Further, the "stages" notion does not fit well even in the sections where it is supposed to apply. Ernest de Selincourt, elaborating on the correlation which Robert Bridges initially suggested between "Sleep and Poetry" and "Tintern Abbey," thus designates the three stages which also correspond to the three stages mentioned in the letter: for Wordsworth's "coarser pleasures of my boyish days" ("Tintern Abbey," 73), Keats's "infant or thoughtless Chamber" and the "laughing school boy" of "Sleep and Poetry" (94); for Wordsworth's lines beginning "The sounding cataract / Haunted me like a passion" ("Tintern Abbey," 76 ff), Keats's second chamber (of "Maiden Thought"), and the "realm" of "Flora, and old Pan" in the poem (96–121); for Wordsworth's "sense sublime / Of something far more deeply interfused" ("Tintern Abbey," 95 ff), the doors of Keats's second chamber beginning to open into dark passages, and the "nobler life" where the poet will find "the agonies, the strife / Of human hearts" ("Sleep and Poetry," 122–56).[23] De Selin-court admits that Keats's second stage (the realm of "Flora, and old Pan") differs noticeably from Wordsworth's, for Keats is involved more in "trivial fancies" than in the natural world; Bridges is not sufficiently confident of the correspondence here to suggest a second-stage passage from "Sleep and Poetry," and he turns instead to *Endymion* (3.142 ff) for a parallel to the passage from the "Tintern Abbey" lines: "The sounding cata-ract, etc." [24] J. Burke Severs emphasizes this lack of correspon-dence between the second stages of Wordsworth and Keats, and he further argues that in "Sleep and Poetry" there are only two stages anyway; in the first Keats considers sensuous joys, but in the second he chooses to deal with suffering humanity.[25]

Garrod and Finney have likewise seen only two stages, the first represented by Flora and Pan, and the second by the charioteer and his vision.[26]

Aside from the critical opinions of readers, the poem's title suggests a twofold subject and sets up the expectation, or at least the possibility, of a twofold structure. This possibility is strengthened when we consider the pseudo-Chaucerian piece, *The Flower and the Leaf,* from which Keats took the motto for his poem.[27] Colvin suggests that this medieval poem provides the "scheme" of "Sleep and Poetry," [28] but he does not identify the scheme more fully. The scheme grows naturally out of the two aspects of poetry which Keats is considering: the poetry of Flora's realm, where one can "sleep in the grass" (102) and "rest in silence" (120), as opposed to the poetry which is the expression of maturity and which is represented by the charioteer (122–54). Keats is describing two stages, and his alternating consideration of these stages gives the poem its structure. A brief examination of *The Flower and the Leaf* suggests that these two stages derive some of their characteristics from the two allegorical figures of the medieval poem—the pleasure-loving Flora, and the constant Lady of the Leaf whose knights strive for noble achievements.

The allegorical Flora, in *The Flower and the Leaf,* is thus described:

> It is Flora, of these floures goddesse.
> And all that here on her awaiting beene,
> It are such that loved idlenes
> And not delite of no busines
> But for to hunt and hauke, and pley in medes.[29]

This Flora is the Lady of the Flower who leads her train of knights and ladies in a dance around the daisy; they praise its beauty whose fragile character is soon proved by its successive exposure to a hot sun, then winds, hail, and rain. All the members of Flora's train are as wilted as the flower after this storm, but they are happily restored by the knights and ladies belonging to the Lady of the Leaf whose company has been sheltered by a laurel tree. They gather soothing herbs for blisters, "the sick fast annointing" (410). Rather than serve Flora, the narrator of the poem chooses, at the end, to serve the Lady of the Leaf, who represents permanence and constancy as well as noble endeavor.

The contrast between the knights who heal the sick, serve the long-lasting leaf, and "seeke honour without feintise or slouth" (549) and those who serve Flora and praise the fading beauty of the daisy is echoed in "Sleep and Poetry." Poetry is described as a noble struggle whose rewards are eternal: like a "strong giant" the poet will seek "Wings to find out an immortality" (82–84); he passes the realm of Flora for a "nobler life" (123); he sees the "great end" of poetry as one that will "sooth the cares, and lift the thoughts of man" (245–47). The poem rises to several peaks such as these in which the poet reaffirms the ultimate, highest aim of poetry. And several times this highest aim is described in opposition to the luxurious realm of Flora which structurally precedes it. For instance, the poet prays that "Poesy" will

> Yield from thy sanctuary some clear air,
> Smoothed for intoxication by the breath
> Of flowering bays, that I may die a death
> Of luxury, and my young spirit follow
> The morning sun-beams to the great Apollo
> Like a fresh sacrifice; or, if I can bear
> The O'erwhelming sweet, 'twill bring to me the fair
> Visions of all places: a bowery nook
> Will be elysium—.
>
> (56–64)

The *or* emphasizes the alternatives: the poet may die a death of "luxury," or, if he can live through the "o'erwhelming sweets," he may move on to greater "visions." There is the implication of risk, and perhaps of choice. If the poet survives the stage of "intoxication," his development can then be seen as a twofold process. These two aspects are developed more fully in lines 96 through 154 where a lengthy section is given to each aspect—first Flora's realm is described (96–121), and then the "Shapes of delight, of mystery, and fear" (138) which appear in the wake of the charioteer's ride (122–54).

Keats almost has something going, structurally. There is a

structure of repetition here in which the two stages of the poetic career are more fully explored with each description of them. This alternating structure is not maintained, however; the long digression on what Keats considered to be the faults of eighteenth-century poetry interrupts (162–247). The digression concludes with a reaffirmation of the "great end" of poetry and seems to be bringing back the antithetical structure again—the alternating consideration of the poetry of Flora and that of the "friend" who soothes man's cares. Perhaps it could be argued that this tirade against the "foppery and barbarism," (182) against the "handicraftsmen" (200) of the preceding age, still continues the structure by describing a lesser sort of poetry first, which is then followed (220–47) by a return to a greater poetry —one that fulfills its true end. But if this is so, the basic antithesis of the poem has shifted the significance of one of its terms: certainly the neoclassic endeavor has very little resemblance to what Keats has, until now, been using as "stage one" of the poet's development—the realm of Flora.

The next section (248–69), with its "simple flowers," birds, fawns, and nothing "More boisterous than a lover's bended knee" (260), perhaps represents another look at the poetry of Flora, that is, at the first stage of the poet's development. If so, then the following section (270–312), in which the poet again affirms his vision of the "end and aim of Poesy" (293), represents a final commitment to this aim. Structurally this commitment probably should conclude the poem, and in a sense it does; some one hundred lines follow, describing the room in which Keats is spending the night. The furnishings—pictures of poets and patriots—seem to be strengthening his resolve.

This twofold, alternating structure has been suggested here because it yields coherence to more parts of the poem than does the three-stages-of-life framework. There are fewer sections left dangling if the poem is seen as a series of alternating reflections on the two aspects of the poet's growth; the two aspects, the two stages, are reminiscent of the two contrasting concerns of the allegorical ladies in the medieval poem, the frivolous Flora and the soothing, enduring Lady of the Leaf. Yet Keats does not use the twofold structure as effectively as he might; the repeated affirmations of the aim of poetry do not develop sufficiently from one affirmation to the next. The result is a structure of mere repetition, rather than repetition with development; such a form results in a poem that seems longer than it is. And this is one way to write a "long poem," of course, although the effect is probably not what Keats hoped to accomplish here.

The three verse epistles in the 1817 volume, like "Sleep and Poetry," show considerable experimentation with structure, and the patterns which Keats uses in them might have been derived from a number of sources. The first epistle, "To George Felton Mathew," is the most tightly constructed of the three; the others, written about a year later in 1816, are more digressive and miscellaneous. Robert Bridges is right when he affirms that the epistle to Clarke is "altogether far the worst" of these verse letters; he fails to see, however, the internal experimentation even in this poem, and, while he says that the other epistles are "well built," he does not elaborate on their construction.[30]

The formal maneuvers in these poems demonstrate the beginnings of the organizational craftsmanship which Keats tests at greater length in *Endymion*. When he wrote the first epistle, the one to Mathew in November 1815, Keats was acquainted with Hunt's precepts for the heroic couplet, but he had no model from Hunt for the verse-letter. Most scholars agree that his models were Elizabethan ones, probably the epistles of Drayton.[31] By the time he attempted this form the second time, with the epistle to his brother in August 1816, Keats had several models written by the man whose poetic theories he had already adopted. Hunt's first epistle, "To the Right Honorable Lord Byron . . . ," appeared in the *Examiner,* 28 April 1816. He published six more during the summer issues. The epistle to Byron is the best and is written in iambic pentameter couplets; for the others he adopts a rollicking anapestic tetrameter couplet which, he explains, is better suited to "chattering." [32] After he begins chattering, Hunt allows the structure of his poems to become more casual also, and casual to such an extent that, in his epistle to Charles Lamb, he admits he must arbitrarily cut off the mythological digression which is threatening to overwhelm the epistolary limits.[33] Keats, following his master for the time being, similarly liberalizes the demands he had earlier placed on this form.

Keats's most likely Elizabethan model, Michael Drayton, wrote several verse epistles to his friends. In addition, he wrote a series of imaginary epistles, "Englands Heroicall Epistles"; these are arranged in pairs, the first one in each pair being an inquiry of some famous figure to a loved one, and the second a reply to it. Keats may have read both the familiar epistles and "Englands Heroicall Epistles." He could have found in the latter—as well as in many other sources—some use of the parallel structure which becomes so significant in his own work. Keats's first epistle, however, written to George Felton Mathew, does not show a close structural imitation of the rather artificial "Englands Heroicall Epistles"; it is instead more reminiscent of the structure of Drayton's less formal verse-letters which were written to his friends. In discussions of Keats's epistles, a few lines of Drayton's epistle to Henry Reynolds are often quoted as a source for the basic situation of the two friends recalling their conversations on poets and poetry:

> My dearly loved friend how oft have we,
> In winter evenings (meaning to be free,)
> To some well chosen place us'd to retire;
> And there with moderate meate, and wine, and fire,
> Have past the howres contentedly with chat,
> Now talk'd of this, and then discours'd of that,
> Spoke our owne verses 'twixt our selves, if not
> Other mens lines, which we by chance had got,
> Or some stage pieces famous long before,
> Of which your happy memory had store.[34]

The first ten lines of the epistle to Mathew very likely owe something to these lines of Drayton. The general structure of this first epistle of Keats, however, follows more closely that of Drayton's epistle to George Sandys,[35] and structure is our main concern here.

In the epistle to Sandys, the two locations of the friends are made to represent opposite possibilities of the subject, poetry. In America, where Sandys is, poetry is still possible; in England, where Drayton is, it can no longer be written. The geographical separation of the two men—that is, the physical basis for writing and sending this letter—establishes the two structural poles of the poem. The immediate reason for Drayton's writing the letter is to advise Sandys about suitable subjects for his poetry while he is traveling; in offering this advice, Drayton neatly manages to bring the two structural halves of the poem together.

After a brief introduction of eight lines, Drayton tells why poetry is scarce in England: the insecure political situation threatens poets who venture onto subjects of national interest, and Drayton himself has suffered from a regal about-face (9–36). Sandys's location, however, does allow for the writing of poetry, and he should continue with his translation of Ovid, which may perhaps restore the exiled English muse (37–58). After this basic contrast, Drayton compares the status of poetry in England first to that of the outcast prophets of Israel, and second to the poets of Greece who have long since been superseded by "the'unletter'd Turke, and rude barbarian trades" (71). Then he brings the past and present together, using this real "barbarian" as a metaphor of the ballad-writer, whose poetry is the only kind to survive now in England; he complains of the "scattered rimes" and the "blind gothish barbarisme" (75–92). Now that he has sufficiently well characterized the two geographical locations, he offers his advice in terms of this characterization of place: Sandys is advised to describe the "naturall bountyes" of America and not to write poems about the "savages," because, Drayton explains, "As savage slaves be in great Britaine here" (93–108). As the poem concludes, the structural poles of the epistle and the reason for sending it meet in the unifying word, *savage.* The poem is strict and restrained.

Structurally considered, Keats's epistle to Mathew, which manifests the same basic devices as Drayton's poem, is his most successful verse-letter. The loose couplets, the feminine rhymes, and the curly diction indicate that Keats is already trying to practice Hunt's prosodic theories, but Hunt offered no general comments on how to build a whole poem; in this one respect anyway, Keats, following consciously or unconsciously Drayton's epistle as model, does very well.

Place is thematically important here as in Drayton's epistle to Sandys. Keats's poem has two sections. In the first part (11–52), the location of the sender is contrasted with that of the receiver of this letter; where Mathew is, in the country, poetry is possible, but where Keats is, in the city, it is not. In the second part (53–93), the answer to the sender's inability to write is suggested by means of imagery which, although hyperbolic and undeserved, is very complimentary to the receiver of the letter: the muse will visit any place where Mathew is, for Mathew is a sort of incarnation of poetry.

The movement of the first section is especially reminiscent of the way Drayton brings the two structural oppositions together in a thought or word that unifies them. After the first ten lines, which celebrate this "brotherhood in song" (2), the results of separation are given. The two places and their poetic significance are described: Keats wishes to follow Mathew "Past each horizon of fine poesy" (11–16); but this is impossible in "this dark city" (17–34); only some "flowery spot" can be visited by the muse (35–50). This opposition of the country and the city is subtly blurred, however; even in the "dark" city, Keats imagines "bright processions" (29) beneath the moon, and even in the flowery spot the flowers of a day are dying ând the "dark-leav'd" laburnum droops (40–44). There are bright visions, or at least remembered ones, even in the dark city, and there is a solemn atmosphere even in the natural spot which the muse may visit. The last two lines of this section reflect and focus the understated paradox of the preceding lines: "There must be too a ruin dark, and gloomy" (51) to remind one, even among flowers and poetry, of faded life and solemn failures. While the muse will not come to the city, " 'Mid contradictions" (34), yet she will visit a paradox; she will not come to a living, immediate city, but she will visit the remains of a frustrated human endeavor whose ruined presence qualifies the pleasantness of the surrounding flowers. It is true, regrettably, that the wretched adjective *bloomy* of line 52 tends to shatter the reader's perception of how strictly within the epistolary demands this section is unified.

The poet's inability to write, which is the problem described in the first section of the epistle, is given its solution in the second part of the poem (53–93). Keats asks Mathew to help him "find a place" where they can greet the muse and "humanity"; this double endeavor of politics and poetry, probably owing something to the same combination of interests in Hunt's *Ex-*

aminer, is developed briefly by references in the next few lines to patriots and poets. With these considerations of the specific subjects of poems which the two friends may write, their geographical separation becomes less important, or less noticeable; Keats now uses *we* and *our* rather than the *me* and *thee* opposition which prevailed in the first section. When Keats again gives the second person pronoun to Mathew (74–93), it is no longer used to contrast the fortunate Mathew's location with that of Keats in the city. Mathew's "every dwelling" is graced by the presence of the muse (74), because, as the remainder of the poem shows, he is an incarnation of the poetic spirit, and his "travels strange" have taken him from Helicon into various living creatures and finally into the "placid features of a human face" (89). In the logic of the poem the connotations of *place* progress from the geographical to the evolutionary, and thus allow the poet to conclude with an assertion of fruitful friendship a poem which began as a complaint of barren separation. The prosody of this poem may offend the ear, and for this reason one cannot call this piece "good," but its structure shows that Keats could give a completed shape to a work of about one hundred lines.

The other two epistles of the 1817 volume show a greater disorder of over-all structure. As Bate observes, there are images in these poems which are more concrete than those of the earliest verse-letter;[36] the direction of the total poem, however, is less sure. This growing capacity for exact observation and for giving careful statement to a world more "natural" than Hunt's mythologically natural one is, of course, a poetic advance; the image of the dolphin who "sports with half his tail above the waves" in the epistle to George and the long simile of the swan which begins the epistle to Clarke are certainly improvements over the vague landscape of the epistle to Mathew. And although these two later epistles are structurally uncertain, they do show signs of positive experimentation.

The epistle to George, written August 1816, apparently has three parts; lines 1 through 66 tell of the "living pleasures" (67) of the bard; lines 67 through 109 relate the richer pleasures of "posterity's award" (68); the remainder of the poem, after an abrupt break in line 109, seems to be a rather miscellaneous defense of the poet's ability to fulfill the double hope described in the first two parts. There are two structural lapses which slow down and blur the progress of the poem. Lines 53 through 66 are, except for the evening's "diamonds" (58) perhaps, a vague and innocuous restatement of the idea (the "living pleasures") that has already been presented vividly and with the reinforcement of structural artifice in lines 1 through 52. And the last thirty lines of the epistle might as well belong to another poem, so tenuous is the relationship of this descriptive passage to the earlier section.

Written about a month afterward, the epistle to Clarke is even fuzzier in structure, although it contains some effective images and gives appropriate characterization to the poetic forms which Keats says he has learned from Clarke (52–72). This collection of lines apparently falls into two groups—those that tell what Keats has been reading with his friend (1–77) and those that tell of Keats's attempt to fulfill the poetic aspirations derived from this reading (78–132). There is perhaps some internal shaping to these two sections, but it is hardly evident enough to give the reader a sense of progression, suspense, or climax. Perhaps there is a climactic movement from the more frivolous reading—"Armida's bowers" of Tasso (30–31)—to the more patriotic, politically focused conversations with Hunt—"The wrong'd Libertas" (44). And perhaps this same movement is traced again as the poem progresses from Spenser's "vowels" through the larger structures of sonnet, ode, and epic and concludes with the "patriot's stern duty" discovered by the muse of history (56–72). Again, there is an internal shape in lines 84 through 96—the movement of a day, from the sun's rising to Cynthia's appearance. These structural controls give some internal shape to the poem, but no over-all relationship of parts is clear.

Considered as experiments, however, "To My Brother George" and "To Charles Cowden Clarke" are far from total failures. Although the over-all structure of both poems is uncertain, brief sections of each do demonstrate some formal artistry. The most successful of these internal structures occurs in the first fifty-two lines of the epistle to George. It is hard to believe that Keats was not consciously arranging the progression and repetition of details here. Structurally there are two parts: lines 1 through 18, and 19 through 52. The second part repeats and develops into an imaginative vision the descriptive details of the natural landscape observed in the first part.

As James R. Caldwell has pointed out, Keats is describing in these lines, as well as in "I Stood Tip-Toe" and perhaps in "Sleep and Poetry," the associationist idea of a poetic vision. It is a train of spontaneous images stimulated by a beautiful natural scene or a work of art. Caldwell suggests that a reader should not expect such episodes to have any very coherent structure. The poet on such occasions is in a "bardic trance." Caldwell finds the origins of this concept in associationist psychology, with which Keats was undoubtedly familiar. Hunt, Wordsworth, and Hazlitt were associationists to some extent; Keats refers to associationism specifically in his letters, and he owned works of Locke and Addison. Also, as Caldwell points out, associationism was the accepted psychology at this time, and it was especially popular in David Hartley's version, *Observations on Man.* All of these writers, whether poets or philosophers, asserted that the imagination, in response to a stimulus, called up trains of visual images which were sometimes only indirectly related to the object or landscape before the observer.[37]

Caldwell emphasizes the oblique relationship between the visionary images and the immediate scene or object. He also emphasizes the lack of structure within the train of images; observation of a landscape "starts the poet on a spontaneous and inconsequent mental process." Caldwell sees this process at work in some of the early sonnets, and in the epistle "To My Brother George." Speaking of a similar poetic trance in "I Stood Tip-Toe," he observes that Keats first describes the immediate scene; of the subsequent visionary musings, he writes: "What follows then is a running account of these thoughts given, if we take his word, as they came to his passive mind, and connected by no principle save that of chance association."[38] The very free, nearly structureless, quality of the bardic trance is one that some associationists emphasized, and one that indeed seems typical of some of the poems by Keats and others in which this convention is used. The trance convention, as it passed from psychology to literature, certainly carried with it implications of spontaneity and liberty.

There are other implications as well, however. Archibald Alison, an associationist whom Caldwell quotes, asserts that the trains of images correspond somewhat to the scene which stimulates them: "When any object, either of sublimity or beauty, is presented to the mind, I believe every man is conscious of a train of thought being immediately awakened in his imagination, analogous to the character or expression of the original object." Again, Alison observes: "In such cases of emotion, every man must have felt, that the character of the scene is no sooner impressed upon his mind, than various trains of correspondent imagery rise before his imagination." [39] As Alison describes this experience, there is a relationship between the scene and the analogous images which arise in the mind of the viewer. This experience Alison evidently considers to be the usual, normal one. On the other hand, the popular associationist Hartley emphasizes the disorderly, random quality of the images in dreams. He suggests that these characteristics are partly the result of the sleeping state of the dreamer, who has no outward scene by which to correct his fantastic visions; also, an unpleasant condition of the stomach, brain, or the body generally, "will make all thoughts warp their own way, little or much." [40] Addison, while devoting a series of essays in the *Spectator* to the "Pleasures of the Imagination," takes time briefly to observe that among the "pains" of the imagination are those occasions when the mind is disordered, diseased and when "the Fancy is over-run with wild dismal Ideas, and terrified with a thousand hideous Monsters of its own framing." [41] The usual, healthy response of the imagination seems to involve a train of images "analogous" to those observed in nature; the images are not entirely random, but correspond in some way to what the observer has once seen and to what he is immediately observing.

When Addison discusses quite specifically those mental images which arise as the observer sees a beautiful landscape, painting, or statue, this critic holds the traditional view that these images occur in a "set," in a group; the observer has associated these images with one another before, perhaps by chance, and now sees them combined again. Addison emphasizes that a "noble Writer" should have the faculty of retaining, and varying, such groups of images; the writer must "be able to receive lively Ideas from outward Objects, to retain them long, and to range them together." [42] Addison does not greatly stress the writer's freedom to rearrange what he finds in a natural scene. This critic maintains a characteristically balanced view: "we have the Power of retaining, altering and compounding those Images, which we have once received, into all the varieties of Picture and Vision that are most agreeable to the Imagination." [43] If Keats's understanding of the bardic trance and of the mind's mode of operation in response to a landscape owes something to Addison and Alison, the description of a poet's visions will correspond, although with variations, to the preceding description of the scene itself.

This is exactly what happens in the first fifty-two lines of the epistle to George Keats. The poet first describes his rural surroundings, expressing the wish that he might have poetic visions; then, in terms of the same rural environment, he does have these visions. Most of the repeated images occur in the same order in both sections:

In "seasons" (3) the poet's mind is overcast with "heaviness" (1–3).	At "times" (19) poets "Fly from all sorrowing" (20).
He gazes to "dimness" (5) at "sheeted lightning" (6).	For a poet in a "trance" (25), "sheet-lightning" is a portal (29–30).
He wonders if he will ever hear Apollo's song (9).	Trumpets blow whose tones reach only the poet's ear (31–32).
He thinks he sees the lyre (12), the symbol of the poetic visions he desires.	He sees a festival, bright goblets, golden halls, and fair ladies who resemble a "seraph's dream"; i.e., the poet now sees the substance of the visions he had desired (33–42).

He would like to sing a "rural song" (14).	Very dimly, he sees bowers, flowers that would make a poet quarrel with a rose (43–46).

A detail which does not occur in the same order in both sections is the reference to chivalric knights and ladies. The poet concludes the first section with the wish that he might see "the bright glance from beauty's eyelids slanting" (15) and that he might relate a "tale of love and arms in time of old" (18). References to the fulfillment of this hope are intermittent in the second part: the poet sees "white coursers paw," and the "gay knights" tilt (26–28), then sees horsemen gliding (34), and finally the "ladies fair" at a festival banquet (36–37).

The detail of the sheeted lightning is the only one which appears in both sections in very nearly the same form. Its presence is an adequate clue to what is happening structurally; the "seraph's dream" of the second part is but the poet's dream as he lies on the earth, gazing at the "blue dome" (5) above him. Some development and expansion of the second section are to be expected in a flight of the imagination; it would have been pedantic for the poet to have nailed down the structural relationship at each point noisily.

The poet does not get lost in the realm of imagination; he returns to the real by means of the dolphin simile. The image is concrete and represents, as other critics have noted, the progress Keats is making from the flimsy, Huntian mythology toward the images of precise natural observation which are typical of this poet's mature work. The dolphin simile is used structurally to complete the movement and meaning of an entire section; it is rendered even more concrete because of its structural position. Keats is considering arrangement here as well as good lines. The image reverses the visionary movement that has preceded it and so brings the entire section back to the real from which it began.

Keats uses this repetitive structure only internally in the epistle to George; but in "I Stood Tip-Toe," the relationship of stimulus scenery to imaginative vision supplies the framework of the entire poem. Again, details of the observed scene are picked up and developed as the poet's imagination begins to expand:

The poet stands "tip-toe," and notices the "tapering" stems of flowers (1, 5); from his position on the hill there is "wide wand'ring for the greediest eye" (15).

The sweet peas are on "tip-toe" for a flight, and their "taper fingers" are "catching at all things" (57, 59).

He cannot see, but can "Guess where the jaunty streams refresh themselves" (22).

He suggests that one "Linger awhile" where a stream's "hurrying freshnesses aye preach / A natural sermon o'er their pebbly beds" (61–71); "The while they cool themselves, they freshness give" (83).

The stream babbles of its "daughters / The spreading blue bells" (42–43).

If the poet were beside a stream, he would "pray" to see a maiden, and "lead her gently o'er the brook" (93–101).

He asks the marigolds to open their "starry folds," for "great Apollo bids" their praises to be sung "On many harps, which he has lately strung" (47–52).

He calls the moon the "maker of sweet poets" (113–16), and eventually asserts that Endymion, Cynthia's lover, was a poet (192–93); (239–41).

The poet's eagerly grasping imagination is later reflected in the sweet pea's "taper fingers"; he describes, by means of imagination, streams he cannot see; he develops the feminized "blue bells" into a woman; finally, the poet-god, Apollo, becomes later a long meditation on several appropriate myths, especially the "poet" Endymion's pursuit of Cynthia. There is no rigid correspondence here, and Keats does not "moralize," does not draw ethical precepts from nature; as Wasserman has pointed out, by the eighteenth century, people no longer believed that analogies were part of a divine scheme of correspondences.[44] The pattern of repeated images which Keats uses in his trance poems indicates no strict relationship between the external world and the psychological one; the structure becomes a statement of the poetic process, and gives a form simultaneously to both the process and the poem.

Keats also uses this repetitive form in the sonnet, "Keen fitful gusts . . .," but here it is an internal structure only and is not so clearly a poetic trance; the second quatrain does suggest, however, an imaginative coloring of the physical details observed in the first four lines. In the first line "fitful gusts" whisper; in the fifth, the poet does not much feel the "cool bleak air." In the second line the dry winter bushes are "half leafless"; in the sixth, the "dead leaves" rustle. The cold stars are described in the third line; in the corresponding seventh, they begin to resemble "silver lamps" burning. The fourth line tells of the long distance yet to travel; by the eighth line, this distance is becoming less important, because the traveler is beginning to think of the pleasant evening he has just passed in the poet's home, an evening which he describes in the sestet. The repetition is clear, and the development is clear; the same images in the second quatrain become less grim, the coldness and death of the season going nearly unnoticed as the stars become warm lamps.

In this sonnet, in the epistle to George, and especially in "I Stood Tip-Toe," Keats has developed a structure which is almost a formal metaphor of one of the favorite ideas of the romantic poets, the idea that the senses "half create" what they perceive; Wordsworth declares in "Tintern Abbey" that he is a lover

> of all the mighty world
> Of eye, and ear–both what they half create
> And what perceive.
>
> [105–07]

He also suggests in the "Prospectus" to his projected poem, *The Recluse*, that the intellect of man is "wedded to this goodly universe" (52–53); a few lines later in the same fragmentary piece he writes:

The external World is fitted to the mind;
And the creation (by no lower name
Can it be called) which they with blended might
Accomplish: —this is our high argument.

[68–71]

Keats certainly read these lines, since they were printed at the end of Wordsworth's Preface to *The Excursion* in 1814. In Keats's description of a bardic trance, the poet's mind and the landscape create between them the structure of the poem. The mind, wedded to the universe, plays with mental images which reiterate or vary the physical objects of nature. The subjective order reflects and develops the objective order in a series of analogous images that are not rigidly repetitive, but suggestive of a happy exchange between the two orders. Keats's remarks about his "favorite Speculation," made in November 1817, are a prose expression of this same idea:

> The Imagination may be compared to Adam's dream—
> he awoke and found it truth ... we shall enjoy our-
> selves here after by having what we called happi-
> ness on Earth repeated in a finer tone and so
> repeated—And yet such a fate can only befall
> those who delight in sensation rather than hunger
> as you do after Truth—Adam's dream will do here
> and seems to be a conviction that Imagination
> and its empyreal reflection is the same as human
> Life and its spiritual repetition.[45]

Here the correspondence is between the "sensations" of life's happiness and the later "spiritual" repetition; Adam's dream, like the bardic trance, links the visionary world with the objective, "true," one. The correspondence of vision and reality, so confidently affirmed in these remarks, gives an effective coherence to the trance poems of the 1817 volume. As Keats affirms his desire to become a poet, his creative response to the sensory world becomes the fabric of the poetic structure itself.

Notes

1. See for instance Bate, *John Keats*, pp. 59–63; Claude Lee Finney, *The Evolution of Keats's Poetry*, 2 vols. (Cambridge, Mass.: Harvard University Press, 1936), 1:103–14; Amy Lowell, *John Keats*, 2 vols.

(Boston: Houghton Mifflin Co., 1925), 1:123–32; Pettet, *On the Poetry of Keats*, pp. 9–10.

2. See Finney, *Evolution of Keats's Poetry*, 1:38; and Aileen Ward, *John Keats* (New York: Viking Press, 1963), p. 37.

3. Robert Gittings, *John Keats* (Boston: Little, Brown and Co., 1968), p. 55; Finney observes that Keats may have read the notes to either the 1814 or the 1815 edition of Hunt's poem (*Evolution of Keats's Poetry*, 1:72).

4. *Keats Circle*, 1:4–5 / n. 1.

5. Finney, *Evolution of Keats's Poetry*, 1:76–77.

6. Leigh Hunt, *The Feast of the Poets* (London, 1814), p. 26.

7. Hunt, *Feast of the Poets*, p. 102. Hunt's remarks on Wordsworth's principle of a "selection" from the language of ordinary men seem to indicate his acquaintance with the Preface of 1802 in which Wordsworth adds a lengthy passage to the 1800 Preface and employs this word twice, emphasizing the principle. Since Hunt does not stress the idea of *selection*, however, he may have been thinking of the 1800 edition, in which this idea is certainly less apparent. See *Feast of the Poets*, p. 106, and Wordsworth and Coleridge, *Lyrical Ballads. The Text of the 1798 Edition with the Additional 1800 Poems and the Prefaces*, ed. R. L. Brett and A. R. Jones (London: Methuen and Co., 1963), pp. 248–55.

8. Hunt, *Feast of the Poets*, pp. 27, 32–33, 37.

9. Ibid., p. 36.

10. Walter Jackson Bate, *The Stylistic Development of John Keats* (New York: Modern Language Association of America, 1945), pp. 19–28.

11. Leigh Hunt, ed., *Imagination and Fancy; or Selections from the English Poets* (London: Smith, Elder, and Co., 1844), pp. 313–14.

12. Hunt, *Feast of the Poets*, pp. 30–32. Warton suggests that the line, "Save Beares, lyons, and buls . . ." (*Faerie Queene*, 2. 1. 14) should read "Save lyons, beares, and buls, etc." Thomas Warton, *Observations on the Fairy Queen of Spenser*, 2 vols. (London: Printed by C. Stower, 1807), 2:165.

13. Hunt, *Feast of the Poets*, p. 71. Thomas Campbell's *Gertrude of Wyoming*, published in 1809, was praised by the *Quarterly Review* for its affinities with the tradition of Pope. See Upali Amarasinghe, *Dryden and Pope in the Early Nineteenth Century* (Cambridge: at the University Press, 1962), pp. 98–99. Keats mentions the poem once, negatively, in January 1820; see *Letters of John Keats*, 2:243.

14. *Letters of John Keats*, 1:169–70.

15. Sidney Colvin, *John Keats* (New York: Charles Scribner's Sons, 1917), p. 165.

16. Joseph Warton, *An Essay on the Genius and Writings of Pope*, 5th ed., 2 vols. (London, 1806), 1:37, 42, 2, 11.

17. T. Warton, *Observations on the Fairy Queen*, 2:29, 78.

18. Hunt, *Feast of the Poets*, p. 26. Oliver W. Ferguson finds verbal

parallels in Thomas Warton's *The Pleasures of Melancholy* and Keats's "Ode to a Nightingale"; see his "Warton and Keats: Two Views of Melancholy," *Keats-Shelley Journal* 18 (1969): 12–15.

19. Joseph Addison, *The Spectator,* ed. Donald F. Bond, 5 vols. (Oxford: Clarendon Press, 1965), 3:570. For the list of books in Keats's library, see *Keats Circle,* 1:253–60. Keats refers to the *Spectator* directly several times (see for instance *Letters of John Keats,* 2:175 and 188), and probably alludes to it on other occasions; see David Bonnell Green, "Keats and 'The Spectator,'" *Notes and Queries* 2 (March 1955): 124.

20. Lowell, *John Keats,* 1:226.

21. Clarke and Clarke, *Recollections of Writers,* p. 134. Clarke says that Keats describes here "the art garniture of the room." The idea for including such a description in a poem might have been given impetus by Hunt's remark on "An Epistle to a Friend" by Samuel Rogers: "The best thing in Mr. Roger's production appears to me to be his Epistle to a Friend, describing a house and it's [sic] ornaments" (*Feast of the Poets,* p. 46). For instance:

> And here the faithful graver dares to trace
> A Michael's grandeur, and a Raphael's grace!
> Thy Gallery, Florence, gilds my humble walls,
> And my low roof the Vatican recalls!

See Samuel Rogers, *Poems* (London: Printed for T. Cadell, 1827), p. 131. Rogers also describes "Frost the Wizard" borne "on vieweles wings" (p. 135); cf. "Ode to a Nightingale": "on the viewless wings of Poesy" (33).

22. *Letters of John Keats,* 1:280–81.

23. Ernest de Selincourt, ed., *The Poems of John Keats* (London: Methuen and Co., 1920), pp. 406–7.

24. Ibid., p. 407; Robert Bridges, *Collected Essays and Papers,* 10 vols. (London: Oxford University Press, 1929), 4:100–101.

25. J. Burke Severs, "Keats's 'Mansion of Many Apartments,' *Sleep and Poetry,* and *Tintern Abbey,*" *Modern Language Quarterly* 20 (1959): 128–32.

26. Garrod, *Keats,* pp. 28–29 n. 2; Finney, *Evolution of Keats's Poetry,* 1:163.

27. The motto is from the third stanza of *The Flower and the Leaf.* It is quoted here as it appears in the Garrod edition of Keats's poems (p. 51):

> 'As I lay in my bed slepe full unmete
> 'Was unto me, but why that I ne might
> 'Rest I ne wist, for there n'as erthly wight
> 'As I suppose had more of hertis ese
> 'Than I, for I n'ad sicknesse nor disese.'

Experimentation: The 1817 Volume

28. Colvin, *John Keats*, p. 115.

29. This poem was printed in all editions of the collected works of Chaucer from 1598 to 1878. The poem purports to have been written by a woman; the authorship is unknown, and several theories have been advanced, based on textual studies, assigning the poem to various writers. For a discussion, see *The Floure and the Leafe, and the Assembly of Ladies*, ed. D. A. Pearsall (London and Edinburgh: Thomas Nelson and Sons, 1962), pp. 79, 13–20. The lines quoted are 534–38. Further quotations are to this edition and are indicated by line number in the text.

30. Bridges, *Collected Essays and Papers*, 4:140–41. Bridges gives a brief analysis of Keats's fourth epistle, "To J. H. Reynolds," p. 141. Although this last verse epistle is interesting in itself, it is not as important for our purposes here as the epistles of the 1817 volume; at this time Keats had not yet managed to get a long poem going, and his experimentation with the methods of doing so is our main concern.

31. See for instance Finney, *Evolution of Keats's Poetry*, 1:84–85; Colvin, *John Keats*, p. 109. Keats owned a volume of Drayton's poems; see *Keats Circle*, 1:254.

32. "Harry Brown to His Cousin Thomas Brown," *Examiner*, no. 444 (30 June, 1816), pp. 409–10. The text of this poem can also be found in *The Poetical Works of Leigh Hunt*, ed. H. S. Milford (London: Oxford University Press, 1923), pp. 224–25. See lines 5–10.

33. *Examiner*, no. 452 (25 August, 1816), pp. 536–37, lines 59–82; in Milford, ed., *Poetical Works of Hunt*, pp. 233–34, and p. 234 n. 1.

34. *Poems of Michael Drayton*, ed. John Buxton, 2 vols. (London: Routledge and Kegan Paul, 1953), 1:151, lines 1–10. Further references to Drayton's epistles will be indicated in the text.

35. Gittings asserts that the "whole idea and shape" of the epistle to Mathew is based on Hunt's *Politics and Poetics*, Keats producing a poem "on exactly the same pattern" (*John Keats*, p. 56). *Politics and Poetics* is not an epistle, however; while the theme—the contrast of the exigencies of business and the desire to find poetic visions in the country—may be similar in Hunt's piece and Keats's earliest epistle, the "shape" of Keats's poem is not "exactly" that of Hunt's. Finney also suggests, though less emphatically than Gittings, that the "theme" of the epistle to Mathew is based on Hunt's *Politics and Poetics*, which was reprinted in the 1815 edition of *The Feast of the Poets*; see *Evolution of Keats's Poetry*, 1:82–84. Structurally, however, Keats's epistle shows more Elizabethan artifice than can be found in Hunt's poem.

36. Bate, *John Keats*, p. 75.

37. James Ralston Caldwell, *John Keats' Fancy* (Ithaca, N.Y.: Cornell University Press, 1945), pp. 9–26, 53–58, 73–75. For Keats's references to associationism in his letters, which Caldwell points out, see *Letters of John Keats*, 1:246, 251–52, 280.

38. Caldwell, *Keats' Fancy*, pp. 12, 19.

39. Archibald Alison, *Essays on the Nature and Principles of Taste* (Edinburgh: Bell and Bradfute; London: J. J. G. and G. Robinson, 1790), pp. 2, 11. And see Caldwell, *Keats' Fancy,* pp. 65–66.

40. David Hartley, *Observations on Man* . . . , 2 vols. (1749); facsimile (New York: Garland Publishing, 1971), 1:383–85.

41. Addison, *The Spectator,* 3:579.

42. Ibid., pp. 562–63.

43. Ibid., p. 537.

44. Wasserman, *Subtler Language,* pp. 180–84.

45. *Letters of John Keats,* 1:184–85.

III

Endymion

Endymion, in many respects, is not so much a failure as an overstated success. Keats wished to test his powers of invention, and he succeeded only too well in amassing images, episodes, and digressions around the "one bare circumstance" of the Endymion myth. From the beginning, the poem is filled with leisurely embellishment. In book 1, Endymion, melancholy and withdrawn during festivities in honor of the god Pan, is led away by his concerned sister, Peona, to an island bower where he rests and then tells her of his three recent encounters with a strange, surpassingly beautiful goddess; in book 2 he begins his search for her by entering a cavernous, underground world where he stumbles upon the bower of Venus and Adonis and later has a passionate meeting with his unknown love in another bower; in the third book, he continues his quest deep in the ocean, and after hearing the unhappy life story of Glaucus, helps him to resurrect his beloved nymph, Scylla, along with many lovers who have been drowned in storms; in the final book he falls in love with a sorrowful "Indian Maid" who accompanies him in a visionary flight on the backs of winged horses and who in the last few lines of the poem turns out to be his goddess, Cynthia, in disguise. Certainly Keats is here pursuing vigorously the kind of fantastic invention which Addison describes as the "fairy way"; or, he may be thinking of the many bowers and gardens of Spenser which Thomas Warton had praised for being "diversified with many new circumstances." [1] The surplus of visions, caves, and bowers slows the movement of the poem and clogs any suspense. In the four thousand lines of *Endymion*, the sheer amount of invention obscures the poem itself. The theme is fuzzy, if there is one; and the structure is almost buried.

Almost. Perhaps Keats's own rather low opinion of this poem, and the diverse and proliferating interpretations as to its meaning have encouraged the suspicion that the poem's over-all structure is flimsy.[2] Critics who see the poem as essentially a love story, or erotic poem, do not often find much structure in it; and their explanation, for what they do find in theme and for what they do not find in structure, is usually that Keats was a very young man.[3] On the other hand, those offering allegorical interpretations are generally more inventive with regard to structure and often add even more imagination to a poem that suffers already from too much of this quality. The allegorists usually see a fourfold structure in the poem's four books, the hero progressing through several stages or realms before finding ideal beauty or ideal love.[4] Another method of encouraging the structure of *Endymion* to float to the surface is to speak some Jungian incantation over the uncertain mass; then Endymion becomes a "vegetation king," and the four books an illustration of the quaternary, or successive stages of a fertility hero's quest.[5] Still another group of readers sees the main theme as that of the growth of a poet's imagination, and these critics generally resist the temptation to draw neat structural boxes around the stages of the poet's growth.[6] But Jack Stillinger has perceived the real reason for the diversity of interpretations; there is, as he affirms, more than one theme in *Endymion.*[7] Yet, in this thematic jungle, the over-all structure, the all-inclusive and most comprehensive pattern, is the one firm element of the poem. I agree with the assertion of Douglas Bush that "the design of the whole is an organic unit, but the control of particular parts is uncertain."[8] And at least some of these particular parts are also "certain"—are meshed into the design of the whole.

The whole has the shape of success, and the structure is almost a metaphor of happy fulfillment. The formal pattern is essentially the same as the one Keats used in "I Stood Tip-Toe," the poem to which he once gave the title "Endymion."[9] In both poems, a pattern of repeated images implies that dream and reality reflect and reinforce each other. In "I Stood Tip-Toe," and in the bardic trance described in the epistle to George, the description of the real world came first, and the vision followed; in *Endymion*, the vision occurs first, and the quest to realize this vision follows. Whether the hero's quest is for beauty, love, truth, or the assurance that the poetic imagination is valid, the quest does succeed, and the structure of the poem becomes a metaphor of happiness attained. Again, as in the trance poems of the 1817 volume, this structure has the shape of Adam's dream and of his dream's relation to reality: "The imagination may be compared to Adam's dream—he awoke and found it truth." [10] This "favorite Speculation" of Keats often enters into a critic's discussion of the meaning of *Endymion;* I would like to emphasize the structural implications of the remark. Essentially it suggests that experience has two parts and that these two parts mirror one another. The first part—the dream or desire—is greeted by something very much like itself in the "real" world. Although the prolific inventive embellishment threatens to overwhelm the poem, its basic structure, a vision embodied and realized in a quest, remains secure.

There are in fact three visions in book 1 of *Endymion;* and books 2, 3, and 4 reflect, in reverse sequence, the imagery of these three visions. The reversed order perhaps emphasizes that the quest is a mirrorlike image of the dreams which foreshadow it. Whatever may be the ultimate "meaning" of Endymion's quest and of his final union with Cynthia, one meaning is fundamental: his quest—or man's quest, or the poet's quest—will and does succeed. Little boosts of assurance are given to Endymion all along the way, the largest encouragement being that he continues to glimpse his goddess in circumstances resembling those of his initial visions. Endymion's cavernous wanderings in book 2 are structurally related to his experiences in book 1 at the mouth of the cave where a woman's voice calls to him. His adventures beneath the sea in book 3 are related to his vision of Cynthia while he gazed into a well in the first book. And his celestial flight in book 4 is the structural counterpart of his initial heavenly vision which he had described to Peona. This structuring pattern which Keats had utilized in the 1817 volume he attempts to extend in *Endymion* to four thousand lines. As a result, the pattern becomes of necessity rather attenuated, but it does at least secure the quest structure at both ends, and it does reinforce the one theme which is the common denominator of most interpretations: Endymion's adventure is a statement of fulfillment, of final happiness. It has to be; the structure implies that the quest itself is an elaboration and expansion of Endymion's early vision.

As the following examination will suggest, Endymion's adventures, though sometimes digressive, do for the most part follow one another in a kind of climax of confirmation. The confirmation—the fulfillment of his search—is implied in the introductory section of the poem; it continues to be elaborated in the hymn to Pan and in Endymion's conversation with Peona concerning his three visions. This confirmation steadily progresses in book 2 through a cyclic but advancing series of cavernous wanderings which are a development of Endymion's preliminary encounter with his goddess at the cave's mouth in book 1. Endymion's growing faith in the success of his search is contrasted in book 3 with the unlucky Glaucus, this undersea episode complementing and confirming Endymion's book 1 vision of Cynthia in the well. And the climax of prosperous hints rises in book 4 to another vision of Cynthia, a vision which recalls Endymion's first sight of her in book 1. When the Indian Maid finally turns into Cynthia, this event represents the ultimate unity of "dream" and "truth," and this unity has been implied in the very structure of the poem.

In book 1, Keats lays the foundation for the poem's structure. In the introductory section and in the hymn to Pan, the narrator already implies that Endymion's dream will just about have to come true; and the three visions in this book establish the pattern which Endymion's wanderings in the last three books fulfill. The famous first line of the poem is qualified by all the lines that follow it. In a world of history and time, a thing of beauty is not really a joy forever. The next line hints of the only manner in which the thing of beauty remains so: "Its loveliness increases." If it increases, it grows and changes; it is prevented from passing into nothingness, only by continually passing into the present moment. "Therefore," the poet says,

> on every morrow, are we wreathing
> A flowery band to bind us to the earth.
>
> [1.6–7]

The *therefore* is important; something is eternally beautiful only if one is continually, "every morrow," reaffirming it to be so in the particular temporal context. For this reason, the "o'er-darkened ways" are "Made for our searching" (1. 10–11). Things of beauty always must be with us in "shine" or "gloom" (1. 32–33). Endymion must find his goddess even in the depths of the cave, for the occasions of mazed perplexity and wandering are those which test one's understanding of the special beauty hidden in things.

There has been some quibble as to whether "these essences" (1. 25)—which become so dear and indispensable to us—refer to something ethereal and supernatural or to real, earthly, concrete things.[11] At this point in the poem *essences* already refers to the paradoxical conjunction of both the ethereal and the concrete in a thing of beauty. The simile that follows the statement makes this clear:

> even as the trees
> That whisper round a temple become soon
> Dear as the temple's self, so does the moon,
> The passion poesy, glories infinite,
> Haunt us till they become a cheering light
> Unto our souls, and bound to us so fast,
> That, whether there be shine, or gloom o'ercast,
> They alway must be with us, or we die.
>
> [1.26–33]

The trees around the temple are said to become dear as the temple itself; i.e., the concrete, growing, changing thing becomes as dear as the mysterious quality to be found in each as a temple is found in a grove. The climax of the poem confirms this paradox. The final recognition that eternal beauty, if that is what Cynthia is, must be found in the temporal (the Indian Maid) takes place outside the temple, and in the grove. These "essences," then, are both the concrete and the ethereal; the two qualities are one when they are perceived as an "essence."

A little later in his introductory description, Keats again suggests the interpenetration of the ordinary and the supernatural.

45

He describes Latmos, the forest, and the little clearing where the altar is (1. 63–106). A lamb might stray from the "happy pens" of his fellows and become forever lost in this forest; but such a lamb doesn't really lose happiness. He passes "unworried" by wild beasts into the "unfooted plains" and joins the herds of Pan (1. 62–79). In the process of describing the setting of his poem, Keats foreshadows its main action: the culminating happiness to be found even in wandering through "o'er-darkened ways." Again, trees are described as having a special relationship to the heaven they partially hide:

> who could tell
> The freshness of the space of heaven above,
> Edg'd round with dark tree tops?
>
> [1.84–86]

Certainly Keats is managing details carefully here, and he reserves for last—as though it were at last discovered in the heavy forest—the description of the altar. Pan's altar represents that perfect conjunction of the supernatural and the natural.

The hymn to Pan celebrates this conjunction. The meaning of the Pan festival and the meaning of Endymion's wandering which is to follow are perhaps most clearly expressed near the end of the hymn:

> Be still the unimaginable lodge
> For solitary thinkings; such as dodge
> Conception to the very bourne of heaven,
> Then leave the naked brain: be still the leaven,
> That spreading in this dull and clodded earth
> Gives it a touch ethereal—a new birth:
> Be still a symbol of immensity;
> A firmament reflected in a sea;
> An element filling the space between.
>
> [1.293–301]

The paradox suggested here and in the introduction to the poem is that wanderings, strayings, solitary dodgings are exactly the means of arriving at the "unimaginable lodge" of the beauty immanent in an elaborate, temporal world. Also, this stanza perhaps adumbrates the three general areas of Endymion's wanderings: the earth in book 2 ("this dull and clodded earth"), the sea in book 3 ("A firmament reflected in a sea"), and

the sky in book 4 ("An element filling the space between").[12]
During his later quest, Endymion receives in each of these
realms—earth, sea, and air—assurances that the supernatural
"leaven" is indeed present.

After Peona has led Endymion away from the festival and has
comforted him in her island bower, he tells her of the three
visions which he has had; these visions, like the hymn to Pan,
adumbrate the three areas of Endymion's subsequent search. In
his first encounter with his goddess, he embraces her in the sky.
A summary of this vision is pertinent, since many of its details
and images appear again in book 4 where they are more elaborately developed. Recounting the circumstances of his first vision to Peona, Endymion says that he found a "magic bed / Of
sacred ditamy, and poppies red" (1. 554–55) where Morpheus
must have passed, or perhaps "matron Night," or Mercury (1.
559–63). With these thoughts in his head, he falls asleep and sees
first the natural moon, although he personalizes "her" and describes her "passionately bright" shining (1. 591–99). Then
Cynthia herself appears as "that completed form of all completeness" (1. 606). Endymion tells Peona that he saw this vision
while in a trance, while "Spreading imaginary pinions wide" (1.
586); he had difficulty maintaining the vision; he nearly fainted
when the goddess touched him, seemed to dive "three fath-
oms" and was then "upmounted" again (1. 637–41) only to
swoop into "frightful eddies" such as "muster where grey time
has scoop'd / Huge dens and caverns in a mountain's side" (1.
648–50). He is roused again, he again embraces the goddess, and
they continue their lovemaking as they drop to "a warmer air"
and a mountain of the earth (1. 651–66).

After telling Peona about his first vision, Endymion attempts
to explain his new relationship to "a love immortal" (1. 849), or
to whatever it is that the goddess represents. His entire explanation and defense of the relationship is significant, although quite
long (1. 777–849). It begins with a brief answer to a question
very important to Endymion who has seen his visionary love,
but unfortunately has lost her again:

> Wherein lies happiness? In that which becks
> Our ready minds to fellowship divine,
> A fellowship with essence. . . .
>
> [1.777–79]

Endymion goes on to amplify this remark, observing that music and poetry make us step "Into a sort of oneness, and our state / Is like a floating spirit's" (1. 796–97). He suggests that there are also

> Richer entanglements, enthralments far
> More self-destroying, leading, by degrees,
> To the chief intensity: the crown of these
> Is made of love and friendship, and sits high
> Upon the forehead of humanity.
>
> [1.798–802]

Love, in other words, seems to represent a higher happiness than art; it can even be so "delicious" that potential heroes, once nourished by it, sometimes no longer want to serve humanity but instead prefer to "sleep in love's elysium" (1. 816–23). After describing the often unseen but real benefits of human love (1. 826–42), Endymion concludes:

> Now, if this earthly love has power to make
> Men's being mortal, immortal; to shake
> Ambition from their memories, and brim
> Their measure of content; what merest whim,
> Seems all this poor endeavour after fame,
> To one, who keeps within his stedfast aim
> A love immortal, an immortal too.
>
> [1.843–49]

Keats himself described Endymion's remarks on happiness as "a regular stepping of the Imagination towards a Truth"; the passage, Keats affirmed, "set before me at once the gradations of Happiness even like a kind of Pleasure Thermometer." [13] Keats asserts that the passage describes the imagination "stepping" toward "a Truth"; the indefinite article is important—*a Truth* —because the passage does not say what the "truth" is. Keats evidently saw the passage as describing only a process, a way, a means, even though all of the stages or "gradations" are seen at once. Similarly, Endymion does not yet possess truth or happiness, but after recounting his first vision he is eager to justify to Peona his new commitment to something which he does not fully understand—a love immortal.

Endymion's speech is best understood, I believe, if it is seen as his immediate and very excited attempt to defend his new passion. The scale of this "Pleasure Thermometer" is a little clouded with the steam of an overfervent inspiration, but at least two marks on the gradual ascent are clear: Endymion distinguishes between mortal love—the "chief intensity" (1. 800, 797–842)—and the even greater happiness of one "who keeps within his stedfast aim / A love immortal, an immortal too" (1. 848–49). In book 4 the Indian Maid becomes the narrative representation of this mortal love, which, though it is probably responsible for much that is beautiful and good in the world (1. 824–42), has also the power to put to sleep in love's elysium men who might otherwise have helped to "wipe away all slime / Left by men-slugs and human serpentry" (1. 820–21). Earthly love is ambiguous in its effect, Endymion says; it can lull to sleep all ambition to help mankind, even though it also "has power to make / Men's being mortal, immortal" (1. 843–44). Endymion's own ultimate allegiance, he affirms, is to an immortal, to a goddess. He first perceives the degrees of happiness as a result of this vision of Cynthia; his more exact understanding of the claims of mortal and of immortal love becomes the culminating test for him later.

After his impassioned defense of his new love, Endymion describes a second vision to Peona. This vision foreshadows his underwater adventures in book 3. Endymion tells his sister that he has often amused himself by setting small ships on the water of a deep well as though he were "the Neptune" of this "petty ocean" (1. 883–84). One day while he is watching the mirrored shapes of clouds in the well, he sees a "cloudy Cupid, with his bow and quiver" in the depths; then the "same bright face" of his unknown goddess smiles from the clear well (1. 888–96).

During his third encounter, Endymion does not actually see his goddess, but he does hear a voice calling him from a cave. He has been "Straying about, yet, coop'd up in the den / Of helpless discontent" (1. 928–29). He finds a brook which leads him to the mouth of a cave (1. 929–35). It is the "grot / Of Proserpine," he thinks, or perhaps "the cell of Echo" (1. 943–44, 947). From the cave he hears his name called by a voice that describes the cave as soundless except for the "light noise" of his own hand as it combs the mysterious woman's "labyrinthine hair" (1. 967–69). At this he hurries into the cave, but apparently does not explore it fully that day. He breaks off his story and tells Peona that he plans to bear up against sorrow; he wants, he says, "to fashion / My pilgrimage for the world's dusky brink" (1. 976–77).

It is difficult to see why this resolution has been so misunderstood. Colvin thinks that it is a resolution to forego any further thought on these distressing visions and becomes only a "sickly half-assurance after all." [14] And Robert Gittings uses it as evidence that the poem is poorly planned. Keats finished book 1 abruptly, writes Gittings, "with a touch that shows how little logic there was in the poem's construction. Endymion vows to think no more of his strange encounters with Cynthia." [15] But such is not his vow at all; on the contrary, he resolves to set out on a pilgrimage. He renounces gloom, but not the visions. Book 1 ends with the hero's resolving to search the world's "o'er-darkened ways" for the perfect beauty which he has seen in his dreams; the search itself proves to be a fulfillment of these dreams. The "logic" of the poem's construction becomes clear as book 2 is seen in relation to this third encounter of book 1.

The action of book 2 follows closely, especially at first, that of the prophetic cavern encounter at the end of book 1. Endymion finds a spring (2. 53) where a flower becomes a butterfly and leads him to a fountain near a cavern's mouth (2. 84–85). There the mythological personification of water, a nymph, tells him he must "wander far" to find the bosom of his love (2. 96–127). When another voice calls from the cave, Endymion enters its "dusky empire" (2. 224). He has at last begun his search, as he had resolved to do at the end of the first book; at that time he had planned to fashion his "pilgrimage for the world's dusky brink" (1. 977). Just as he was "Straying about," in book 1, yet "coop'd up in the den / Of helpless discontent" (1. 928–29), so he is here experiencing the same puzzling paradox. He is wandering, yet he finds only a "journey homeward to habitual self" (2. 276). The brief metaphorical "den" which described this condition in book 1 has now been expanded into an elaborate cave. Other images—the "marble cold" (2. 265), Endymion's "Chilly and numb" bosom (2. 243–44), and "the deadly feel of solitude" (2. 284)—suggest that this cave is a more detailed exploration of that cave of book 1, which he feared might be the entry to Hell (1. 943–44).

Endymion's progressive realization, in book 2, that his destiny is larger than his own solitary broodings, shows Keats's "invention" operating with considerable structural ingenuity. The hero's cavernous adventures follow a cyclic pattern. After his first period of wandering, he is refreshed in the bower of Venus and Adonis. After the second, he embraces his goddess in the jasmine bower. He is briefly alone in the cave for a third time. Then he overhears the amorous rivers; after he prays for their happiness, he is no longer in the cave, but in the sea. Each episode ends with a prayer and with Endymion having gained a greater understanding of his still mysterious destiny.

His first prayer is to Diana in a cold, lifeless, "mimic temple"; isolated and hungry, he asks to be restored to the green, living earth where he may slake his thirst with the juice of berries (2. 302–32). Soon he finds the green bower of Venus and Adonis, where he eats and receives the promise that he will someday be "blest" (2. 441–55, 573). Although he does not yet know that Cynthia is suffering for love of him, the meeting with Venus and Adonis prepares him for this knowledge. He will not be like Adonis, a fool, who rejected a "heaven dying at his feet" (2. 464). Secure in the hope of future happiness, Endymion may be again alone, but he will no longer be lost; Venus has asked her son to favor him. The gods themselves are arranging his fate.

The second episode (2. 588–669) shows Endymion's growing hope; he hurries on "with unusual gladness" (2. 593). The cave is now full of falls and fountains, briefly taking shapes of living things—trees, birds, and naiads. Cybele's appearance is described in terms perhaps too awesome and terrible to fit well into this passage of increased life and hope. In her character as a fertility symbol, however, she appropriately follows the Venus and Adonis episode, as E. C. Pettet has remarked.[16] Endymion is stronger now, not only because of the nourishment he has received, but because of his new knowledge about his destiny. His second prayer demonstrates his willingness to fulfill this destiny. He bows to Jove, and "Without one impious word" flings himself on the eagle that carries him down into a green bower (2. 653–69). Here he embraces his goddess and discovers that she suffers as much as he does from their thwarted relationship, but his ultimate happiness is reconfirmed as she assures him: "An immortality of passion's thine" (2. 808).

The third episode is largely given to the stories of the two rivers which Endymion overhears; Endymion is solitary only for a few lines. We are told that he "stray'd" (2. 873) out of the bower; after this, he sits down and considers past events, evidently trying to see the pattern or purpose of his life. He does not specifically recall how he related his distress to Peona, justifying his adventure of love at great length; instead he remembers these events as "His sister's sorrow" (2. 898). The sorrow was largely his, but he is now more aware of his sister's sympathetic grief. It is not surprising, then, that the third prayer offered by Endymion in this book is the intercessory one for the unhappy lovers, Alpheus and Arethusa. As the book revolves again to this point in its repetitive structure, Endymion is again delivered from the gloominess of the cave—this time, into the sea. One third of the hero's quest has now been completed; the promise offered by the mysterious voice which called from the cave in book 1 has been narratively expanded into climactic episodes as Endymion more fully explored a landscape reminiscent of his earlier encounter. Structurally as well as thematically, dream and reality are coming closer together.

They continue to move closer together as Endymion, in book 3, pursues his quest on the ocean floor. His experiences here are the counterpart of his brief second vision which he related to Peona in book 1; on that occasion he caught only a glimpse of his goddess as her image was reflected in the depths of the well. His vision of her at that time was preceded by a "cloudy Cupid" (1. 889). Similarly, in book 3, Endymion sees the moon only through the heavy atmosphere of water, and, the narrator says, at the special instigation of Love, the "winged Chieftain," (3. 100–11). Cynthia appears only as the heavenly satellite here—not as a female deity—and so Endymion does not perceive that the moon and his goddess are manifestations of the same reality. He is now at his farthest remove from Cynthia. Although he does not directly meet her, he finds Venus and Cupid in Neptune's court. The gods of love, rather than Cynthia herself, preside over the action.

Although the third book is linked, by means of Endymion's foreshadowing vision, to the broad structure of the poem, the long story which Glaucus tells concerning his unhappy love affair with Scylla does constitute a rather bulky digression. Internally, this book is the most poorly managed of the four. The only significant action in it seems to be the resurrection of the drowned lovers, accomplished by Glaucus and Endymion; and this action, of course, does push forward one of the poem's themes, suggesting that Endymion is continuing to advance in human sympathy. In book 3 he translates into action the substance of his intercessory prayer for Alpheus and Arethusa at the end of the second book.

An apologist would be taxed to the limit of his enthusiasm if he tried to make every line of the long story of Glaucus "fit" significantly into Endymion's experience, even though Endymion's search is to some extent reflected in the life of Glaucus. He was once, like Endymion, "a lonely youth" (3. 339); he fell in love with the nymph Scylla and pursued her with no success (3. 399–410); he found comfort in Circe's "bower" (3. 465–66), as Endymion did in the bower of Venus and Adonis, but Glaucus was deceived by Circe whereas Endymion received promises from Venus that he would someday be blest (2. 573). After his discovery that Circe has transformed men into beasts, and after she transforms Glaucus himself into an old man, he finds the dead Scylla (3. 477–638). Nothing in Endymion's experience is ever quite so terrible; he never ventures suddenly onto the corpse of Cynthia. Even though their lives are parallel to some extent, Endymion's experience has never been as discouraging or as desperate as that of Glaucus; Endymion never meets Circe, and his mysterious goddess, unlike Scylla, does embrace him occasionally.

Perhaps the most significant thing about Endymion's relationship to Glaucus is that their lives have been so dissimilar. Glaucus never received three encouraging prophetic visions concerning his life's destiny and his love, Scylla. Unlike Endymion, who manages, on the strength of his visions, to bear up against sorrow, Glaucus finds his agony too fierce to bear (3. 410). Perhaps it is not entirely his fault that he seeks out the magical aid of Circe and as a result of "fierce temptation" is overcome by her (3. 412–52). Circumstances did not favor Glaucus; his experience did not fulfill his hopes. Endymion's dreams have moved closer and closer to fulfillment, but for Glaucus a "specious heaven was changed to real hell" (3. 476). In a poem which affirms fulfillment by testing the "o'er-darkened ways," the presence of Glaucus is especially appropriate; he seems to represent the darkest challenges, the gloomiest possibilities for missing out on happiness. After reading book 3, we feel that if even Glaucus is at last brought mysteriously into the large harmony of fulfillment, surely Endymion's ultimate happiness is secure, for he has been constantly receiving encouragements.

After the worst has happened to Glaucus, after Circe's curse turned him into an old man who must bury the dead Scylla, his hope for renewed life and love begins more and more to resemble Endymion's. Just as the water nymph told Endymion that he had to "wander far" to find the bosom of his love (2. 123–27), the mysterious scroll tells Glaucus that all will be well if he *"Scans all the depths of magic"* and *"explores all forms and substances / Straight homeward to their symbol-essences"* (3. 695–700). His intellectual explorations are perhaps the counterpart of Endymion's physical wanderings. If Glaucus pursues *"Most piously"* the task of burying the drowned lovers, a chosen youth will at last *"consummate all"* (3. 701–10).

The man who turns this hope into reality, Endymion, is a figure whose very life seems to symbolize the relationship of hope to fulfillment; his quest so far has been demonstrating that dream incidents and images reappear and develop even in the darkest wanderings. Appropriately, Endymion, after helping Glaucus, is himself given yet another assurance of bliss, even though, at the bottom of the sea, he is "far strayed from mortality" (3. 1007). As a group of Nereids carry the swooning Endymion, he sees written in starlight: *" 'tis done— / Immortal bliss for me too hast thou won"* (3. 1023–24). On the ocean's floor, where he has no encounters with Cynthia, and where he helps a man who was given no heavenly assistance in wooing his love, Endymion hears his goddess promise him immortal bliss. He and Glaucus have successfully met the challenge of searching out the very darkest ways.

In book 3, then, the resurrection of the drowned lovers by

Endymion and Glaucus indicates a further extension of Endymion's developing sympathy; in addition, this resurrection, and the renewal of youth for Glaucus, suggest that promises and prophecies are, in the world of the poem, fulfilled. Glaucus follows the admonitions written on the scroll, and the hope of rescue is fulfilled when Endymion visits the sea in pursuit of his own promised happiness. The action of book 3, and even the apparently digressive tale which Glaucus relates about himself, help to reinforce the theme which has been at work in the very pattern of the poem: dreams mirror and fulfill themselves in action. The special significance of book 3 is that it suggests the working out of this fulfilling process even when there is least expectation of its accomplishment. Even Glaucus finds fulfillment, and even Endymion, whose goddess is present in this book only as a distant and watery moon, receives here another encouraging communication from her which is the structural counterpart of the shadowy glimpse he saw reflected deep in the well in book 1.

The final merging of dream and fulfillment occurs in book 4; here Endymion's heavenly flight reflects and develops the implications of his first vision in book 1, and a transformation of the Indian Maid into Cynthia completes the coalescence of the natural and the supernatural, of reality and vision, of "truth" and "dream"—the dream which had given to Endymion, as it gave to Adam, his first vision of the woman he was to love. Before the happy denouement, however, Endymion and the reader face some surprises. The biggest surprise is the sudden presence of the dark-haired Indian Maid whose beauty captures Endymion's desire.

He is torn between this new passion and his still vigorous love for Cynthia. After the dark maid sings about her vain effort to find comfort by traveling with Bacchus, Endymion is completely smitten, saying "I've no choice; / I must be thy sad servant evermore" (4. 300–301). Mercury suddenly appears, strikes the ground with his wand, and two horses spring up which carry the Indian Maid and Endymion on a prolonged heavenly flight. Here Endymion dreams of Diana, then wakes and sees her; he experiences confusion over his simultaneous attraction to her and to the Indian Maid at his side, and after the Indian Maid's horse drops "hawkwise to the earth" (4. 512), Endymion finds himself in the "Dark Paradise" of the melancholy but soothing "Cave of Quietude" (4. 538–48). While suspended in this place of numb content, he evidently hears, but does not see, the festive preparations for Diana's wedding (4. 556–613). When his horse arrives on solid ground, Endymion proposes to give up Cynthia and live with the Indian Maid; she mysteriously refuses, but when they meet again, she changes suddenly into Cynthia—an alteration which takes care of Endymion's conflicting emotions, and which evidently represents the resolution of whatever oppositions may remain at this late point in the poem. As this summary indicates, the ending of the poem is asked to carry almost more weight than can be packed into it; Endymion's load of passion, vision, conflict, and discouragement seems to evaporate too rapidly as the poem whisks its characters away with a "happy-ever-after" ending.

Perhaps the best explanation for the sudden ending and for much of the involved action of book 4 is given by the Indian Maid just after her transformation. She says, now as Cynthia, that her "foolish fear" and then "decrees of fate" hindered their union; she continues:

> And then 'twas fit that from this mortal state
> Thou shouldst, my love, by some unlook'd for change
> Be spiritualiz'd.
>
> [4.991–93]

It is appropriate that Cynthia says this just after discarding the guise of the Indian Maid, who represents, in this last book, the final test which Endymion must face. It is through his anguished relationship with the Indian Maid that Endymion is "spiritualized"; she becomes the narrative testing of his affirmation, made just after his first vision in book 1, of a commitment to "A love immortal, an immortal too" (1. 849). If Endymion had been able to forget Cynthia, and if he and the Indian Maid had been able to live happily on earth together, then he would have slept "in love's elysium" (1. 823) and would have been unfaithful to his passionate vision of an "immortal" spouse. He would have been content with only half of what was promised to him. The final test, and the completion, of Endymion's spiritualization is the subject of book 4, and this spiritualization does not mean

that he leaves the real world forever. He in a sense has both the
Indian Maid and Cynthia, since they are one, and as Cynthia
says to Peona, "we shall range / These forests" (4. 993–94).
What is finally accomplished at the end of the poem is that
union of the natural and the supernatural which the hymn to
Pan celebrated and which Endymion's wanderings, since they
have mirrored his initial visions, have been implying all along.

The structure of book 4, although heavily embellished with
action, dreams, and songs, continues to develop the pattern
established by the first three books; book 2 developed narratively Endymion's experience at the mouth of the cavern in
book 1, and book 3 developed the implications of his vision of
Cynthia in the well. In book 4, the imagery which was first
introduced as part of Endymion's heavenly vision in book 1,
now develops into full-blown actions, and the brief metaphors
of this former dream develop into events and characters. Mercury, for instance, was merely a thought in Endymion's mind
in book 1 as he puzzled over the sudden appearance of flowers
in his favorite retreat; he wondered if Mercury's wand could
have caused the growth of blossoms (1. 554–64). In book 4 Mercury becomes an important character, appearing at a crucial
moment. Endymion has heard the Indian Maid's song and has
fallen helplessly in love, feeling compelled to be her "sad servant" (4. 301). As Endymion courts her in delight and disbelief,
he hears the words *"Woe! / Woe! Woe to that Endymion! Where
is he?* (4. 320–21). These words are strongly reminiscent, as
Bernard Blackstone has pointed out, of God's "Where art
thou?"—the question that confronts Adam after his fall.[17] As the
frightened couple tremble, Mercury appears and produces the
winged steeds which carry them into the sky. Mercury's sudden
interruption of the love-making resembles his appearance to
Aeneas when the divinely chosen founder of Rome is dallying
away his time with Dido in Carthage.[18] Just as Mercury, in
Virgil's epic, spurs Aeneas on to his higher calling, so Mercury
here interrupts the strongly tempted Endymion and gives him
the opportunity to renew his desire for Cynthia in a visionary
flight.

Instead of simply saying that the couple on horseback grew
drowsy and saw visions, Keats develops here many of the circumstances of Endymion's vision of Cynthia in book 1, and by

so doing suggests that the visionary flight in book 4 is fulfilling the implications of the earlier one. "Sleep," now becomes a character whereas he, along with Mercury, had been in Endymion's mind as a possible cause of the new flowers; Endymion in book 1 thought that perhaps "Morpheus / In passing here his owlet pinions shook" (1. 559–60). In book 4, "Sleep" is in dreamy flight, "slumbering towards heaven's gate" to hear the "marriage melodies" before sinking down to "his dusky cave again" (4. 370–84). This cave, and the "Cave of Quietude" (4. 512–48) into which Endymion falls in despair when the Indian Maid melts from his embrace, recall the "dens and caverns" mentioned briefly by metaphor in book 1 (1. 647–50). The flying horses of book 4 are associated with poetic inspiration; the only thing that can follow their flight, the narrator observes, is the "buoyant life of song," the "pinions" of inspiration (4. 348–56). Endymion's earlier dream, in which he spread "imaginary pinions wide" (1. 586), is here developing into an extended test of his love for Cynthia, a love which he first discovered during his vision in book 1.

Endymion almost fails this test. That the Indian Maid—or Cynthia, disguised as the Indian Maid—plays the role of a temptress is made clear by the narrator before Endymion sees her. It would have been better for Endymion to have vanished into the air than to fail now; "Is Phoebe passionless?" asks the narrator, and he asserts that she is "fairer far" than this new woman (4. 52–57). It is "impious" for Endymion to love the Indian Maid (4. 87). As soon as Endymion sees the dark stranger, he confesses that his feelings for her conflict with the earlier allegiance of his soul; his heart is cut in twain (4. 89–97). When he asks the dark maid to be his "nurse," he realizes that he is going against decrees of fate (4. 117–22). Then, on the winged horses, Endymion can compare the sleeping Indian Maid with his own goddess, now recognized as Diana for the first time (4. 429–33). His conflict here is carried to a very acute extreme, perhaps even a preposterous extreme. After seeing Diana in his dream, he awakes, while still on the drifting steed, and sees the same people and the same festive preparations which were in his dream: he "Beheld awake his very dream" (4. 436). The transformation of dream into reality has been his experience throughout his adventures as his initial visions were mirrored and developed in his wanderings. Now, however, just when his vision of Cynthia turns into Cynthia herself, his desire wavers because he "feels the panting side / Of his delicious lady," the Indian Maid (4. 440–41). While Phoebe looks on, he asks forgiveness, but he kisses the Indian Maid (4. 449–55). Yet this is not the worst. Endymion despairs (4. 506) upon seeing the Indian Maid fade from his grasp, and he completely gives in to the "Happy gloom" of the "Cave of Quietude" (4. 512–48).

The conflict which Endymion experiences as his affection alternates from Cynthia to the Indian Maid indicates that he is not yet "spiritualized"; he is still not seeing his destiny whole, but perceiving it as divided and in pieces. This failure results in his confusion during the flight, his despair in the Cave of Quietude, and his continuing discouragement afterward. Since Diana seemed to be only a "shadow" as he kissed the Indian Maid (4. 445–46, 455–56), and since the Indian Maid's hand "melted from his grasp" (4. 509) as the moon rose, Endymion might have guessed that the two women were really one. The same failure of perception continues while he is in the Cave of Quietude. It is a "Dark Paradise," a happy place, but one where nothing is seen; its happiness depends on deprivation. While he is in the state of despair represented by the cave, he does not see the "vision" of preparations being made for Cynthia's wedding: "Alas, no charm / Could lift Endymion's head" (4. 556–57). He does, however, hear the song which is being sung by the "skyey mask, the pinion'd multitude" (4. 558); we are told, as his steed plunges to earth, "More / Endymion heard not" (4. 611–12). He hears for a brief time, but because of his despair, he does not see.

When he returns to earth again, he continues his vain attempt to be satisfied with only part of his destiny. He seems to be doubting the possibility of the fulfillment which his adventures have all along been promising to him. Endymion resolves to live with the Indian Maid in a pastoral contentment; he says, "let our fate stop here" (4. 633). He affirms that Pan will allow them to live in peace and love (4. 634–36), but this oversimplifies Pan's relation to men as it was described in the hymn in book 1; Pan opens mysterious doors (1. 288) and gives the earth "a touch ethereal" (1. 298). Pan represents the conjunction, or interpenetration, of the natural and the supernatural, of the ordinary and the visionary. Endymion is now willing to recognize only half of Pan's significance, to see only the natural, earthly beauty of the Indian Maid, even though he had once insisted to Peona that his desire was for a "love immortal." After his long and taxing adventures Endymion seems to be losing his courage; he is apparently willing now to settle for less than he once desired. He even falsifies his experience in his effort to find some peace. It is not true that Endymion has been "Presumptuous against love," though he asserts he has; he has made every effort, until now, to find the goddess whom he loves. His soul has not conspired against its proper glory, nor has he "starv'd and died" while he "bent / His appetite beyond his natural sphere" (4. 638–48). When he bent his appetite beyond his natural sphere, entering the cave in book 2, he was nourished in the bower of Adonis. But he proceeds to renounce the three realms of his wanderings:

> Caverns lone, farewel!
> And air of visions, and the monstrous swell
> Of visionary seas! No, never more
> Shall airy voices cheat me to the shore
> Of tangled wonder.
>
> [4. 651–55]

These realms are those which he has just explored: caverns in book 2, the sea in book 3, and the "air of visions" in book 4. But these adventures did not "cheat" him; they confirmed his hope. In the cavern of book 2, he was promised by Venus that he would be "blest" (2. 573), and later in the jasmine bower he embraced his love, thereby confirming the voice which, in book 1, had called to him from the cave (1. 964–69). In book 3 during his oceanic adventures, which reflected and developed his musings and his vision beside the well (1. 888–96), he helped even the unlucky Glaucus to fulfill the demands and promises of a prophetic scroll, and Endymion himself received a reassuring message written in starlight. Once again, in book 4, while he soared through the "air of visions," he beheld his goddess Cynthia in the same heavenly surroundings which first gave rise to his desire in book 1. His adventures, although they have been involved and at times disheartening, did not deceive him; true, his quest has been a long ordeal, but it has continually provided hints and promises of ultimate happiness. The narrator himself asserts that Endymion, by denouncing the realms of his search, is only making excuses, only striving "by fancies vain and crude to clear / His briar'd path to some tranquillity" (4. 722–23).

When the Indian Maid insists that she and Endymion cannot live together (4. 752–53), Endymion loses both worlds. He has turned his back on Cynthia, and his love for the mortal beauty cannot be consummated. He loses both worlds, because he was trying to be content with only half of what destiny had promised him. Peona's words, as she comes upon the sad couple, clarify the impasse which Endymion has reached. She urges him to be happy at the prospect of returning to his kingdom and of having the Indian Maid as his queen (4. 816–17). Peona misunderstands the causes of Endymion's melancholy and thinks that the explanation lies in his being "too happy" at what she has told him:

> Now, is it not a shame
> To see ye thus,—not very, very sad?
> Perhaps ye are too happy to be glad:
> O feel as if it were a common day.
>
> [4.817–20]

Although Peona does not understand the real cause of Endymion's grief, her advice here is very appropriate, and the reminiscence of Wordsworth exactly identifies Endymion's failure; in the "Prospectus," published with *The Excursion* in 1814, Wordsworth had written that the "discerning intellect of Man / When wedded to this goodly universe" will find "Paradise" to be "A simple produce of the common day" (47–55). Endymion is unable to perceive the conjunction of "Paradise" and the "common day" which the very structure of his adventures, and of the poem, have been confirming. He cannot see his visions in the arduous wanderings he has experienced; he has not been "spiritualized" sufficiently to see the supernatural "leaven" which fills all things, as the hymn to Pan affirmed; he has assumed that he can have either "mortal love" or "a love immortal," but not both. He cannot see that the two halves of his experience are really one, that his visions in book 1 and his adventures later are mirror reflections of each other.

Endymion is suffering from a loss of perception which is evidently caused chiefly by his own disbelief in what destiny has promised to him. Preparing to meet the Indian Maid for the last time, his state of mind still resembles what it was in the Cave of Quietude where his numb discouragement had made him only half aware of the preparations for a heavenly wedding. In a "deathful glee," he laughs "at the clear stream and setting sun," and at "nature's holy countenance" (4. 944–48). He feels he has a right to complain:

> I did wed
> Myself to things of light from infancy;
> And thus to be cast out, thus lorn to die,
> Is sure enough to make a mortal man
> Grow impious.
>
> [4. 957–61]

Again, there are echoes of Wordsworth; Endymion asserts that he has "wed" himself to things of light, implying that he used to recognize and experience the union between his hopes and the world, used to be "wedded to this goodly universe." He is now so discouraged, so "drown'd / Beyond the reach of music" (4. 963–64), that his senses are numb as they were in the Cave of Quietude; and so he fails to hear the choir of Cynthia (4. 964–65).

Only after Endymion again asks to know his fate, which he has been denying, is he allowed to see that the Indian Maid and Cynthia are one; meeting the Indian Maid in the grove, he says: "Sister, I would have command, / If it were heaven's will, on our sad fate" (4. 975–76). It is significant that he directs these inquiries about his fate to the Indian Maid. He has often received assurances from visions of his goddess, from a voice in a cave, or from messages written in starlight, but he has not until now sought information from the Indian Maid about his destiny. He has instead insisted that he would deny his destiny in order to live with her: "By thee will I sit / For ever: let our fate stop here" (4. 632–33). Now, however, when he thinks he has lost everything, he is again willing to take up the reins, to resume his commitment to "heaven's will."

For the first time, Endymion sees in the Indian Maid not merely mortal love and mortal beauty, but a representative of heaven's will; until now, he had perceived only a conflict between heaven's will and his passion for the dark maid. Keats does not say why Endymion can suddenly perceive in mortal beauty the representative of his heavenly destiny. Endymion's new perception is perhaps the "unlook'd for change" by which he is "spiritualiz'd" and made ready for a union that represents the interpenetration of vision and reality. Endymion's dream came true, like Adam's, only after he awoke and was able to perceive its substance in reality.

Endymion, although the whole poem may be better than the sum of its parts, is a beautiful narrative embodiment of the confidence which Keats, early in his career, shared with Wordsworth, a confidence that the mind of man is wedded to the universe and that external reality complements the hopes and dreams of human beings. Keats incorporates this idea into the structure of *Endymion* by again using a formal pattern similar to that of the bardic trance; dream and reality reflect each other in a pattern of repeated images. With this pattern as its framework, the over-all structure of *Endymion* is quite coherent, the three preliminary visions in air, water, and cavern, being developed in reverse order in the last three books. The pattern not only holds together Keats's first long poem, but reinforces the significance of Endymion's involved quest; his adventures progressively confirm as truth the very substance of his dreams.

Notes

1. Addison, *The Spectator,* 3:570; T. Warton, *Observations on the Fairy Queen,* 2:29.

2. In the published preface to *Endymion,* Keats speaks of its "mawkishness," and in the rejected preface he says that his "steps were all uncertain" while writing this poem. See *Poetical Works,* pp. 64, xciii. His thoughts were "very low" as *Endymion* neared completion, and he expected to gather only the "fruit of Experience" from this effort; later he tells Shelley that his mind was "a pack of scattered cards" when he wrote *Endymion.* See *Letters of John Keats,* 1:168; 2:323.

3. E. C. Pettet, *On the Poetry of Keats,* p. 153; Lowell, *John Keats,* 1:455, 460; Gittings, *John Keats,* pp. 163–64; Newell F. Ford, *"Endymion*—A Neo-Platonic Allegory?" *ELH* 14 (March 1947): 64–76; John Jones asserts that in *Endymion,* "Sex has to go it almost alone," but he also complains that the poem is flawed by its "pseudo-spirituality." See his *John Keats's Dream of Truth* (London: Chatto and Windus, 1969), pp. 137, 185–86.

4. Among those offering an allegorical interpretation are: Harold Bloom, *The Visionary Company,* 2d ed., rev. and enl. (Ithaca and London: Cornell University Press, 1971), pp. 368–78; Bridges, *Collected Essays and Papers,* 4:80–93; Douglas Bush, *Mythology and the Romantic Tradition in English Poetry* (New York: Pageant Book Co., 1957), pp. 94–97; Colvin, *John Keats,* pp. 171–75; Finney, *Evolution of Keats's Poetry,* 1:293–319; Milton A. Goldberg, *The Poetics of Romanticism* (Yellow Springs, Ohio: Antioch Press, 1969), pp. 75–87; Bruce E. Miller, "On the Meaning of Keats's *Endymion,*" *Keats-Shelley Journal* 14 (Winter 1965): 33–54; John Middleton Murry, *The Mystery of Keats* (London: Peter Nevill, 1949), pp. 119–23; de Selincourt, ed., *Poems of John Keats,* p. xl, pp. 416–17; Clarence D. Thorpe, *The Mind of John Keats* (New York: Oxford University Press, 1926), pp. 48–62; Jacob D. Wigod, "The Meaning of *Endymion,*" *PMLA* 68 (September 1953): 779–90.

5. See Bernard Blackstone, *The Consecrated Urn* (London: Longmans, Green, and Co., 1959), pp. 122, 134; Robert Harrison, "Symbolism of the Cyclical Myth in *Endymion,*" *Texas Studies in Literature and Language* 1 (Winter 1960): 538–54. The mythic elements may have entered *Endymion* by way of Arthurian romance, since Keats's library included a "History of King Arthur," probably Malory's version, published in 1816; see *Keats Circle,* 1:259, and n. 65.

6. Walter H. Evert, *Aesthetic and Myth in the Poetry of Keats* (Princeton: Princeton University Press, 1965), pp. 89–174; Stuart M. Sperry, *Keats the Poet* (Princeton: Princeton University Press, 1973), pp. 90–116. Glen O. Allen, "The Fall of Endymion: A Study of Keats's Intellectual Growth," *Keats-Shelley Journal* 6 (Winter 1957): 37–57. Helen E. Haworth, "Keats and the Metaphor of Vision," *Journal of English and Germanic Philology* 67 (July 1968): 371–94.

7. Jack Stillinger, *The Hoodwinking of Madeline* (Urbana and Chicago: University of Illinois Press, 1971), pp. 14–30. Stillinger further observes that "thematic unrelatednesses" are quite common in long poems; see p. 26.

8. Bush, *Mythology and the Romantic Tradition,* p. 94.

9. See *Letters of John Keats,* 1:121 n. 6.

10. Ibid., pp. 184–85.

11. The allegorists generally argue that *essence* here and *fellowship with essence* in the pleasure thermometer speech (1:779) refer to the transcendent; see for instance, Finney, *Evolution of Keats's Poetry,* 1:297–99. Others interpret the word to mean the concrete, physical

thing; see Pettet, *On the Poetry of Keats,* pp. 155–60, and Newell Ford, "The Meaning of 'Fellowship with Essence' in *Endymion,*" *PMLA* 62 (1947): 1062–76. Stuart Sperry points out that *essence,* along with several other words (*abstract, ethereal, sublime*) sometimes has a quite specific scientific meaning for Keats; see his *Keats the Poet,* pp. 30–56. H. W. Piper suggests that Keats's use of the word *essence* is often close to Wordsworth's idea—as expressed in *The Excursion* especially—of an animating principle in individual, specific things; see his *The Active Universe* (London: University of London, Athlone Press, 1962), pp. 159–64. George Bornstein discusses the scientific and popular meanings which *ethereal* had for Keats in "Keats's Concept of the Ethereal," *Keats-Shelley Journal* 18 (1969): 97–106.

12. For this suggestion I am indebted to Professor James Benziger of Southern Illinois University.

13. *Letters of John Keats,* 1:218.

14. Colvin, *John Keats,* p. 182.

15. Gittings, *John Keats,* p. 139.

16. Pettet, *On the Poetry of Keats,* p. 170 n.

17. Blackstone, *Consecrated Urn,* p. 181.

18. Mercury appears twice to Aeneas near the end of book 4, lines 265–76 and 560–70; for a recent English verse translation which supplies approximate line numbers, see *The Aeneid,* trans. C. Day Lewis (New York: Doubleday and Co., Anchor Books, 1953), pp. 89, 98.

IV

Hazlitt, and New "Axioms" in *Isabella*

The poems which Keats wrote after *Endymion* begin to show more effective ways of elaborating the "bare circumstance" into a well-developed narration. For the next narrative, written in the early spring of 1818, he departs from the challenges of the "fairy way" of writing and chooses as his subject the "natural" story of Isabella and the pot of basil. This choice, along with the new poetic theory and practice which he begins to develop late in 1817 and in 1818, indicates a heavy influence of Hazlitt's critical ideas. Keats's growth as a narrative poet owes much to his understanding of such words as *gusto* and *intensity*, and he probably borrows these concepts from Hazlitt. In Keats's use of these words, and in his remarks about Milton and Shakespeare, he evidently begins to perceive some new formal elements. With *Isabella*, he learns to "lyricize" the narrative; that is, he shapes and contours the action by means of imagery. During a climactic event in a poem, he crowds a line, or a stanza, with vivid adjectives or metaphors; during the less excited moments of the narration, the description of characters and events is less vivid, and the metaphors tend to be brief or conventional. The imagery "rises" and "sets" in a way that emphasizes the narrative elements of suspense, climax, and resolution. Although observations on Keats's vivid imagery are a critical commonplace, his use of imagery to reinforce the progression, through time, of narrative events, has been largely overlooked. With *Isabella* he begins to use imagery narratively; it structures the poem's action.

Hazlitt, and New "Axioms" in *Isabella*

Since Keats's new approach to narration is at least partly the result of his acquaintance with Hazlitt and with his criticism, a look at some of the significant concepts in Hazlitt's criticism will be useful before examining *Isabella*. Some caution is prudent; in some instances Keats may have been simply agreeing with Hazlitt, as Bernice Slote observes, rather than borrowing.[1] And yet, Keats may have sometimes supposed that an independently developed idea of his own was being met by a similar one of Hazlitt's even though the poet's idea was itself derived from a previous reading of Hazlitt's criticism. That is, Keats had the opportunity to meet twice most of Hazlitt's ideas which become important in the poet's vocabulary. Some of these, certainly, must have seemed "almost a Remembrance,"[2] because they were.

Keats probably first met Hazlitt at Hunt's house in the fall of 1816;[3] however, Keats could have become acquainted with Hazlitt's use of the word *gusto* as early as 20 August 1815, when the critic's Round Table article on Milton's versification appeared in the *Examiner.* Speaking of Milton's *Paradise Lost,* Hazlitt writes that "Dr. Johnson and Pope would have converted [*Milton's*]vaulting Pegasus into a rocking-horse." Keats probably read the article; in "Sleep and Poetry" he paraphrases this remark, asserting that the neoclassic poets "sway'd about upon a rocking horse, / And thought it Pegasus" (186–87). There is no indication, however, that he responded in 1815 to Hazlitt's praise, in this article, of Milton's gusto and of his "intense conceptions of things."[4] Hazlitt does not define gusto very adequately here, so perhaps for this reason the word made little impression. In a later article, of May 1816, Hazlitt more fully explains the word and relates it to other important terms of his critical vocabulary: *invention, imagination,* and the *intense.*[5] But again, there is no evidence that Keats had at this time taken notice of the concept which was later to become so important for him. He was paying more attention to the appearance of Hunt's epistles in these spring and summer issues of the *Examiner* and was already so intent on getting a long poem started, so eager to test his powers of "invention," that he probably failed to notice the opposition which Hazlitt observed between the discursive character of "dramatic invention" and the concentrated, intense character of gusto.

When the two-volume publication of Hazlitt's *Round Table* appeared in 1817, Keats evidently read these essays with more care than he had given them in the *Examiner.* In September he says he is reading *The Round Table;* in November, as he rereads Shakespeare, he remarks on the "intensity" of the poet's conceits; and in December, he reviews Kean's acting, praising its gusto.[6] He attends the critic's lecture series on the English poets given early in 1818.[7] His annotations on *Paradise Lost,* made during the winter, 1817–18,[8] show a critical perception of structure which is evidently derived from remarks he has heard Hazlitt make about Milton. Although he did not attend Hazlitt's lectures on the English comic writers, delivered in November, December (1818), and January (1819), he was acquainted with them and quotes an extended passage from one of them in a letter of January 1819.[9]

During this period of fairly continuous encounters with Hazlitt's thinking, Keats begins to respond to his reading—of Milton and Shakespeare, especially—with observations on the relationship of the parts of a poem to the whole, or with comments that show a perception of how the imagery is contoured and molded to give emphasis to character and action. Rather than responding merely to the isolated loveliness of a line or idea, Keats observes the "surrounding atmosphere" of imagery, or its "progress." His judgments of lines or works are specific and critical, rather than vaguely enthusiastic. To a great extent he develops his own criteria and vocabulary for making these judgments, and yet they closely resemble some of Hazlitt's observations. Especially important for Keats's growing sense of the complexities and opportunities which a long poem offers are Hazlitt's use of the related words, *gusto* and *intensity,* his advocation of "natural" subject matter, and his several cautionary remarks on certain kinds of "invention."

The meaning that accrues to a word when Hazlitt employs it varies according to the other concepts with which it is contrasted in any given context, just as Hazlitt's evaluation of an author varies with the writers which he is comparing to each other. In his Round Table essay "On Gusto," he defines the famous word which had acquired a history even before Hazlitt used it; *gusto* had advanced from a synonym for *taste* to a concept sometimes related to the sublime.[10] According to the first sentence of Hazlitt's essay, "Gusto in art is power or passion defining any object." This assertion does not go far toward a definition, although *power* is another word often linked to the sublime.[11] But within the first paragraph, at least two qualities of gusto are made explicit: "There is hardly any object entirely devoid of expression, without some character of power belonging to it, some precise association with pleasure or pain: and it is in giving this truth of character from the truth of feeling, whether in the highest or the lowest degree, but always in the highest degree of which the subject is capable, that gusto consists."[12] That is, *gusto* must, first, give the essential character of a thing, and, second, do so in the highest degree. As a principle for the evaluation of a work's merit, this idea is much tougher and more incisive than any offered by Hunt. It divides and judges; some works fall on one side, some on the other.

Hazlitt immediately proceeds to demonstrate its workability. The coloring in Titian's paintings gives the essential character of its female figures: "his bodies seem to feel," and the objects in his pictures leave an impression "distinct from every other object." By the same criterion, "Vandyke's flesh-colour, though it has great truth and purity, wants gusto. It has not the internal character. . . . The eye does not acquire a taste or appetite for what it sees. In a word, gusto in painting is where the impression made on one sense excites by affinity those of another."[13] With these remarks, and their approximation to a definition of synesthesia, the relationship of the first requirement of gusto (giving the essential character of a thing) and the second (giving this in its highest degree) is clarified and elaborated; Claude's landscapes provide an example of a failure in this respect: "they lay an equal stress on all visible impressions; they do not interpret one sense by another; they do not distinguish the character of different objects as we are taught, and can only be taught, to distinguish them by their effect on the different senses."[14] To fail to represent the essential character of a thing in its highest degree is to fail, really, to represent its essential character at all, and to fail, as a result, to meet the demands of gusto. The "equal stress" which Hazlitt sees Claude giving to "all visible impressions" can be contrasted with Keats's efforts in his later poems to vary the intensity of his imagery behind different characters and actions.

When Hazlitt begins to explain just why Claude's paintings lack gusto, he moves from a definition of this word in itself to a definition of it in relation to other important terms of his critical vocabulary; he notes that this painter's eye lacked "imagination; it did not strongly sympathize with his other faculties." A little later in this essay, Hazlitt further clarifies the meaning of gusto by using it with several important concepts:

> The infinite quantity of *dramatic invention* in Shakespeare takes from his *gusto*. The power he delights to show is not *intense*, but *discursive*. He never insists on anything as much as he might, except a quibble. Milton has great *gusto*. He repeats his blow twice; grapples with and exhausts his subject. His *imagination* has a double relish of its object.[15]

In order for an artist to represent the essential character of any object in its highest degree, he must develop his subject as fully as it requires and insist on it until its manifold possibilities are realized. The meanings of the two words, *gusto* and *intensity*, are intermingled, and Keats as well as Hazlitt sometimes uses either term to refer to about the same thing. When Hazlitt speaks of intensity here, he seems to be indicating a little more fully and explicitly the means of achieving gusto.

In the Round Table article on Milton's versification, Hazlitt remarks that Milton has gusto, and then goes on to explain that this poet "forms the most intense conceptions of things." [16] Earlier in the same essay, Hazlitt speaks of Milton's style in terms that evidently describe this quality of intensity, or the capacity to form the most intense conceptions of things: "He adorns and dignifies his subject to the utmost. He surrounds it with all the possible associations of beauty or grandeur, whether moral, or physical, or intellectual. He refines on his descriptions of beauty, till the sense almost aches at them." [17] To achieve intensity, the author must surround the subject with all possible associations, moral and intellectual ones included; either Keats accepted this idea from Hazlitt or firmly agreed with it, because he made some efforts to realize it in *Isabella*.

As an impetus to the poet's imagination, Hazlitt in another Round Table essay recommends the "natural" subject; the literary examples which he gives indicate that the natural subject is generally one involving strong emotion. For instance, because of this "trust in nature," the author of *The Flower and the Leaf* is able to describe the woman's pleasure at hearing the nightingale, a pleasure that "still increases and repeats and prolongs itself, and knows no ebb." That is, the essential character is here developed to its highest degree, because of the imagination's having taken its impulse from a natural subject—the very moving song of the nightingale. Giving further illustrations, Hazlitt remarks: "So Isabella mourns over her pot of Basile, and never asks for any thing but that. So Lear calls out for his poor fool, and invokes the heavens, for they are old like him. So Titian impressed on the countenance of that young Neopolitan nobleman in the Louvre, a look that never passed away." [18] Titian has captured the look that does not pass away —the essential character of the man's expression; he has given the painting gusto, as Shakespeare has given it to Lear and Boccaccio to Isabella, because his imagination developed and exhausted its subject; the subject lent itself well to the purpose by being not a fanciful, mythological one, but a natural one which can be found in the "real" world of conflict, of personal and social interaction. Hazlitt in these passages from *The Round Table* is relating to each other the important concepts of *nature, imagination,* and *gusto.* And Keats's understanding of them is evidently similar to Hazlitt's. He reads *King Lear* again in January 1818 and writes a sonnet on the occasion: he chooses this play's "fierce dispute / Betwixt damnation and impassion'd clay" rather than "golden tongued Romance" ("On Sitting Down to Read King Lear Once Again," 5–6, 1). [19] He makes a somewhat similar distinction in the choice of his next narrative subject, writing the simple story of Isabella's grief, rather than developing an elaborate narrative texture of myth and fairies as he had done in *Endymion.* A natural subject, not a fanciful one, sets the imagination on toward the artistic achievement: gusto.

Notice that Hazlitt's typical and constant praise of Shakespeare suffers a qualification with regard to gusto: "The infinite quantity of dramatic invention in Shakespeare takes from his gusto. The power he delights to show is not intense, but discursive." When Hazlitt compares the dramatist with Milton, Milton comes out ahead as the intense artist whose imagination insists on, develops, and exhausts its subject. Yet, from his remarks on *King Lear* as exhibiting the imaginative fullness to be found in a natural subject, we must conclude that Hazlitt does credit Shakespeare with gusto; he makes only the qualifying assertion that the *amount* of dramatic invention lessens the gusto.

In an early article in the *Examiner*, Hazlitt had used the word *invention* in a more positive context; writing in 1814 on Wordsworth's *Excursion*, the critic had said that this poem "is certainly deficient in fanciful invention." He went on to explain that the poet in this work "has scarcely any of the pomp and decoration and scenic effect of poetry: no gorgeous palaces nor solemn temples to awe the imagination. . . . we meet no knights pricked forth on airy steeds; no hairbreadth 'scapes and perilous accidents by flood or field." [20] Hazlitt implied here that if the poem had these things—palaces, temples, knights, and perils—it would be improved. While he allows these remarks to stand with little change in the 1817 publication of *The Round Table*, in his lectures a few months later he identifies the failure of *The Excursion* more precisely: Wordsworth, he says, "cannot form a whole. He has not the constructive faculty. He can give only the fine tones of thought, drawn from his mind by accident or nature, like the sounds drawn from the Aeolian harp by the wandering gale.—He is totally deficient in all the machinery of poetry." [21] Hazlitt has abandoned his earlier suggestion that a little "fanciful invention" would improve *The Excursion*. This poem already has too much of something, perhaps too much of the random impulse of the author's own personal thought. What the poem needs is focus, structure, wholeness. Hazlitt's judgments vary here from his earlier ones, probably because of the context of these remarks. He is looking at Wordsworth now after having distinguished the relative merits of greater poets: Shakespeare and Milton, Chaucer and Spenser. He had praised both Chaucer and Spenser, but he had praised them for different reasons, observing the former's "depth of simple pathos and intensity of conception, never swerving from his subject," in contrast to Spenser's "exuberance of fancy" and his capacity as "an inventor of subject-matter." [22] Such comparisons and distinctions perhaps helped to qualify the value for Keats of *invention* as a proliferation of subject matter. Keats had been too preoccupied in *Endymion* with amassing from one circumstance fanciful material sufficient to fill four thousand lines.

In the remarks which we have examined Hazlitt does not tell anybody how to write a long romantic poem in a few easy lessons. But he does suggest certain means of getting a poem going: repeat, develop the subject to its highest degree, give it all possible associations, exhaust it, take a double relish in it. The structural implications here could have been valuable to a young poet whose acquaintance with critical ideas, before he met those of Hazlitt, had encouraged a vague enthusiasm for "coy loveliness."

Probably the most important of the structural ideas for which Keats owed something to Hazlitt is that of developing fully the imagery of a poem. In the frequently quoted letter, written to John Taylor in February 1818, Keats relates his axioms for poetry:

> 1st I think Poetry should surprise by a fine excess and not by Singularity—it should strike the Reader as a wording of his own highest thoughts, and appear almost a Remembrance—2nd Its touches of Beauty should never be half way thereby making the reader breathless instead of content: the rise, the progress, the setting of imagery should like the Sun come natural to him— shine over him and set soberly although in magnificence leaving him in the Luxury of twilight—but it is easier to think what Poetry should be than to write it—and this leads me on to another axiom. That if Poetry comes not as naturally as the Leaves to a tree it had better not come at all.[23]

David Perkins has very rightly observed of Keats's first axiom that any "study of the development of Keats's poetry will focus on the progressive fineness of the excess. For the excess, at least the potentiality for it, seems present from the beginning." [24] Keats himself, I think, has in these remarks to Taylor indicated how he plans to make the excess fine. Hazlitt had suggested that Milton took a "double relish" of the objects he was describing, that he exhausted his subject; Keats is saying the same thing here, as he asserts that the "touches of Beauty" should be fully developed. Similarly, in his annotations on his copy of *Paradise Lost,* Keats writes that Milton "in every instance pursues his imagination to the utmost." [25]

Along with the idea of completing, fully developing, a subject, is the structural concept of giving the imagery contour, of making it rise and set. Paul Sheats has suggested that Keats's odes demonstrate a kind of rising and setting imagery in their pattern of approach and withdrawal.[26] Keats also exploits the structural implications of his axiom in his narrative poetry, making the imagery "rise" by increasing the number of metaphors within a stanza or by extending a metaphor over several lines. The effect varies; sometimes the emotion of a stanza is heightened and sometimes a climactic suspense is built up in the course of several stanzas. Keats's use of imagery for narrative purposes deserves special emphasis, because he is often thought of as being only a "spatial" poet, and one who is inept when he must describe a temporal sequence of actions. A recent critic, John Jones, insists that Keats is unable to make a narrative "linear and temporal" and that when he tries to do so, he is usually, in Jones's words, "bad" and "verbal." [27] While this kind of failure is true of much of *Endymion,* it is not so in *Isabella.* When Keats speaks of the progress of imagery, of its rising and setting, he is not just happening upon a striking metaphor. As he says to Taylor, he is enunciating an "axiom" which he has apparently not discovered much before now and certainly has never practiced with any skill before the poem *Isabella.* The imagery of *Endymion* rises, but never sets; or perhaps it would be more accurate to say that it never really rises very far. The combined effects of the description and metaphor give a perpetual and tiring glaze to the poem; the level lushness is uniform and does not vary with the events narrated. In *Isabella, The Eve of St. Agnes,* and the remaining narrative poems or attempts at them, the imagery is employed structurally. It rises for the emotional peaks; it glows vividly behind certain characters and provides for others only a very subdued background.

In addition to the "axioms" in which Keats articulates his concept of rising and setting imagery, some of his comments on

Shakespeare and Milton indicate a more mature understanding of how to develop a "bare circumstance" into a poem. Several of these comments seem to be recalling Hazlitt's observations on "intensity." In a letter to John Hamilton Reynolds, Keats enthusiastically observes of Shakespeare's sonnets: "they seem to be full of fine things said unintentionally—in the intensity of working out conceits." The second quatrain of sonnet 12, which he quotes to illustrate his remark, demonstrates rather well Hazlitt's assertion that to achieve the intense in a poem, the writer must bring to bear all possible associations and must repeat the blow, taking a "double relish" in the object described:

> When lofty trees I see barren of leaves
> Which erst from heat did canopy the herd,
> And Summer's green all girded up in sheaves,
> Borne on the bier with white and bristly beard.[28]

Whether Shakespeare managed these lines "unintentionally," as Keats suggests, or deliberately arrived at their total effect, they do characterize autumn by demonstrating its association with summer, and they do this twice, the third and fourth lines repeating the idea of the first two, although with a different metaphor. When Keats praises Edmund Kean's acting in his review of December 1818, he does so in terms which show that the same basic criteria are being applied: "There is an indescribable gusto in his voice, by which we feel that the utterer is thinking of the past and the future, while speaking of the instant." [29] Whether writing or acting, the artist must bring to the moment associations which are beyond it in order to give it intensity, or as Keats says here, gusto, using synonymously the two terms which were not always kept entirely distinct even by Hazlitt himself.

One of the "possible associations" by which a writer can increase the intensity of his work is that of contrast. The Shakespearean quatrain, whose intensity so impressed Keats, utilizes this element, heightening the sense of change and loss by describing autumn largely through metaphors that contrast it with summer. Perhaps Keats's remarks on the "Magnitude of Contrast" in his annotations to *Paradise Lost* are related to the complex of ideas which Hazlitt associated with intensity, although the poet may be thinking more independently here. This principle of contrast is one which becomes structurally important in his later poems: "There is a greatness which the Paradise Lost possesses over every other Poem—*the Magnitude of Contrast*, and that is softened by the contrast being ungrotesque to a degree. Heaven moves on like music throughout. Hell is also peopled with angels; it also moves on like music, not grating and harsh, but like a grand accompaniment in the Base to Heaven." [30] Keats notices the "progress" of the contrast. Hell's music, like Heaven's, "moves" throughout; the magnitude of the contrast is partly a function of its contributing to a sustained narration. Although Keats does not incorporate the principle of contrast into the actual structure of a narrative until *The Eve of St. Agnes,* he does utilize the idea briefly in *Isabella.*

While Keats was still enunciating the foregoing concepts and still in the process of exploring their implications, he began to incorporate some of them into *Isabella.* There is general agreement that *Isabella* demonstrates several kinds of improvement over *Endymion,* although there is no consensus about the success of the total result. Keats himself, by the autumn of 1819, considered the poem "mawkish" and "weak-sided"; and yet, as he began working on it in February 1818, he was evidently developing the axioms which he sent to Taylor in the same month.[31] Some of these new axioms are given a first test in this poem, even though Keats was not entirely satisfied with the results of his efforts. Of the new structural elements, the most evident are the "natural" theme, the rising and setting of imagery, and the awkwardly deliberate attempt to increase the poem's intensity by surrounding its main action with all "possible associations," including moral and intellectual ones.

Keats had written to Taylor that "if Poetry comes not as naturally as the Leaves to a tree it had better not come at all." Since he had been reading *The Round Table* a few months before announcing these axioms, it may be that he is here recalling Hazlitt's remarks on the "natural" story, the story of real people in real distress, as providing a very strong impetus to the imagination. Hazlitt had in the Round Table essay mentioned the story of Isabella, along with *King Lear,* as examples of such a natural theme. When Keats, in February, heard Hazlitt suggest a metrical translation of some of the "serious tales in Boccaccio and Chaucer, as that of Isabella,"[32] the combined associations of serious and natural may have encouraged him to see in this tale a subject for a poem that would excel in qualities opposite those of the fanciful *Endymion.*

Keats is careful to distinguish between "old Romance," and the more realistic approach which he is taking in recounting the story of Isabella. While Isabella and the nurse are digging up Lorenzo's body, stanza 49 briefly explains:

> Ah! wherefore all this wormy circumstance?
> Why linger at the yawning tomb so long?
> O for the gentleness of old Romance,
> The simple plaining of a minstrel's song!
> Fair reader, at the old tale take a glance,
> For here, in truth, it doth not well belong
> To speak:—O turn thee to the very tale,
> And taste the music of that vision pale.
>
> [385–92]

Jack Stillinger has emphasized with great justification the distinction which Keats makes, in this stanza, between the "wormy circumstance" which he is describing, and the "old Romance" as Boccaccio told it; the "realistic" details, which Keats adds to the "old tale," result in an "antiromance."[33] I agree, essentially. I think, however, that Keats may be using realism here for purposes other than, or at least in addition to, the purposes of writing a tough-minded, "modern" antiromance. Hazlitt had said that the imagination responds more readily and fully to a subject such as the nightingale's song in *The Flower and the Leaf,* Isabella's sorrow, or Lear's distress; with such a natural or "realistic" subject, the poet is more likely to achieve the desired quality of gusto. Keats suggests, in the quoted stanza, that "gentleness" does not really belong to the story of Isabella as he sees it. If the poet's imagination truly responds to such a "natural" subject, he will achieve an intensity, a gusto, that will emphasize and reinforce the painful sense of grief. Keats proceeds therefore to develop the "wormy circumstance"; the poet must "linger at the yawning tomb" when he is describing a grief like Isabella's. Hazlitt had said that she "mourns over her pot of Basile, and never asks for any thing but that." Her preoccupation with grief is extreme, Hazlitt suggested; Keats makes this preoccupation even more emphatic by rendering in detail Isabella's gruesome actions. His goal is to allow his imagination fully to respond to the subject; his goal is, ultimately, gusto.

By choosing the story of Isabella as his subject, Keats probably felt that he could more nearly embody his new axioms in the narrative. The modeling of the imagery, in particular, demonstrates intensity; it is a "fine excess," a progressive rising and setting of vividness. The imagery as the poem begins is of a subdued or conventional character. Keats demonstrates here more control of his emotional range than he did in *Endymion;* he can write pianissimo as well as forte now. The early events of this story move slowly, much more slowly than in Boccaccio's tale. This early "love idyll," as M.R. Ridley designates it, is expanded to consume nearly one-third of the poem whereas Boccaccio uses only one-seventh of his story to tell of the developing romance.[34] The first eleven stanzas are slow-moving, but they describe an awkward, painful, and very slow courtship. Perhaps Keats succeeds too well here in presenting the gradual stages of the consummation of this affair, but the slow pace is certainly appropriate to the events being narrated. Also appropriate, and for the same reason, are the dearth of any but the briefest or most conventional imagery in the first four stanzas, the contorted and intellectualized "conceits" of stanzas 5 through 9, and the relaxed description of the fulfilled happiness of the lovers in stanzas 10 and 11. Very subdued, implied metaphor is used twice in the first stanza, and both uses are so conventional as scarcely to seem metaphorical: Lorenzo is a "palmer in Love's eye," and the lovers suffer the typical "malady" (2, 4). Perhaps the last line contains a slight figurative jostle in the phrase "to each other dream," (8) since, in conventional expression, one generally dreams "of" people rather than "to" them. In the second stanza the subdued description yields two very brief, and tentative, comparisons in "than noise of trees or hidden rill," (14) and this is as near as the stanza comes to metaphor. The imagery of religion and of sickness is again applied briefly in the third stanza; Lorenzo is constant as "vespers," and he waits for Isabella's step with "sick longing" (21, 23). The fourth stanza allows a few short phrases—"bow to my delight," "breathe not love's tune," and "Honeyless days" (27, 30, 32)—to lift the description of the longing lovers into the intensity of figurative language. On the whole, these stanzas are, for Keats, or for anyone, very subdued writing. No wonder the action seems to be moving very slowly; the languishing pace of events, emphasized by the unexcited language, very aptly introduces these shy lovers who suffer silently, afraid to express their love.

The imagery "rises" at stanza 5, however. That is, the metaphors are no longer conventional, but instead vividly unique, and even a little peculiar. The new metaphorical tone of the poem here is not entirely successful, but, in a sense, these bizarre and "mixed" metaphors are appropriate. Isabella's cheek "Fell sick within the rose's just domain" (34). This is certainly a roundabout way of saying that her complexion paled. But this contorted metaphor, and those used in stanza 6 to describe Lorenzo's difficulty in expressing himself, do yield an uneasy tension to the poem here and thus emphasize the events being narrated; the "ruddy tide" of Lorenzo's blood "Stifled his voice," and "Fever'd his high conceit of such a bride" (44–46). Perhaps Keats has merely achieved the bizarre in stanza 9 when he describes the lover's first kiss: Lorenzo's lips "poesied with hers in dewy rhyme" (70). This is, however, a courageous improvement over the "slippery blisses" of Endymion's meeting with Cynthia in the jasmine bower (2. 758). Certainly, since such intellectual contortions do not characterize the imagery of the rest of *Isabella,* their isolated presence here indicates either that they came "unintentionally" as appropriate to the lover's awkward struggle for expression, or that they are a quite deliberate effort to keep the poem very clear of the sensuous sentimentalism of *Endymion.* Perhaps Keats exaggerates here; in order to avoid the bog of bathos, he attempts to keep the lover's meeting on the level of the Elizabethan conceit, and he achieves an extravagant perplexity of thought and sense.

The intensity of the imagery drops for two stanzas, 10 and 11, which describe the fulfillment of this love. There are no longer any strained contortions of metaphor; the lovers leave each other as "Twin roses by the zephyr blown apart" (74). The "honey'd dart" (78) of which Isabella sings is a return to conventional imagery of love. The single metaphor of stanza 11—dusk, taking "from the stars its pleasant veil"—is rhetorically repeated (82, 84), a device which succeeds in once again slowing the pace of the poem and diminishing the excitement of the preceding stanzas. The imagery of stanzas 1 through 11 has risen and set, rather well.

It rises in intensity again after Lorenzo is slain and diminishes after Isabella's pot of basil is taken away. The imagery of the digression, beginning at stanza 12, which interrupts the narration of events in order to describe the greedy brothers, gives some presage of the fierce and prolonged intensity that will characterize the language after the brothers have performed the murder. Already, even in this background description of their pride and greed, the imagery "prolongs and repeats itself"; the metaphorical language continues through several lines of stanzas 14 and 15, rather than briefly touching the subject as it had in the early stanzas of the poem. After the series of digressions culminating in the apology of stanzas 19 and 20, the narrative continues in a very low key. Perhaps the "whisper" of Isabella's footstep and her "musical" laugh (196, 198) must technically be considered metaphorical language, but sharply distinctive figurative language occurs only on two occasions in stanzas 21 through 26: when the brothers of "cruel clay" decide to "Cut Mercy with a sharp knife" (173–74) and when they encourage Lorenzo with deceptive words to accompany them before the sun counts "His dewy rosary on the eglantine" (187–88)—a speech which the narrator refers to as "these serpents' whine" (190). Stanzas 21, 23, and 26 are bare, and so allow the brief flashes of metaphor in this section of the poem to give sinister emphasis to the plotting of Isabella's brothers.

In stanza 27 metaphor builds subtly by means of brief epithets—"murder'd man," "straiten'd banks," and "dancing bulrush" (209, 211, 212); after the slaying, figurative language becomes thick and intense, simile and metaphor meshed together to describe Lorenzo's soul: "It aches in loneliness—is ill at peace / As the break-covert blood-hounds of such sin" (220–21). As a result of the murder, the event that brings Lorenzo and the brothers together in one act, he and they are alike: both ill at ease, because of the crime. The moment is tense, and the language is tense.

When the brothers tell their sister she must no longer hope, the imagery rises to personification—not very successfully, but it still rises. The personifications of Hope, Selfishness, Love, in stanzas 29 and 31 represent perhaps a deliberate effort to raise the level of intensity beyond the language used to describe the slaying in stanza 28. They also recall the personification of Mercy—in stanza 22—used to emphasize the cruelty of the plot which has now succeeded in producing such sorrow for Isabella. Deliberate or not, these personifications are not the way to get there; the artificiality of this device diminishes rather than increases the emotional intensity of the events.

Keats does manage a peak, however, even though the personifications fail to contribute to its structure; he does so by extending and developing his similes, piling them up for several lines. All but the first line of stanza 34 build up to a terror that is not designated until stanza 35, when we are finally told: "It was a vision" (273). The imagery that describes Lorenzo's appearance, his voice, and eyes, in stanzas 35 through 37, is heavy and vivid. Probably the climax of intensity arrives in the famous simile used to describe Lorenzo's fading away into the darkness:

> The Spirit mourn'd 'Adieu!'—dissolv'd and left
>   The atom darkness in a slow turmoil;
> As when of healthful midnight sleep bereft,
>   Thinking on rugged hours and fruitless toil,
> We put our eyes into a pillowy cleft,
>   And see the spangly gloom froth up and boil.
>
> [321–26]

Nothing like the prolonged imagery of these stanzas has been used before in the poem, and the effectiveness of it here is partly a result of the restraint shown by the poet earlier. Keats is learning how to phrase a narrative, how to strike the keys harder when the music needs to be louder.

Although there is one five-line simile, in an aside to the reader (354–58), there are very few metaphors during the relation of Isabella's digging into the grave and salvaging the head to nourish a basil plant. The gruesome details are described at some length, but quite simply; in fact, the dearth of metaphorical language here perhaps increases the tension during this episode. When Isabella and the nurse at last reach Lorenzo's body, when they feel "the kernel of the grave," the narrator carefully emphasizes: "And Isabella did not stamp and rave" (383–84). Her failure to stamp and rave is reinforced by the narrator's similar refusal to indulge in excited language; instead he simply relates the "wormy circumstance," his unexcited tone reinforcing the sense of numb, morbidly helpless grief.

A few metaphors occur while Isabella tends the basil pot, but they are very brief. For example, we see "the jewel, safely casketed" (431), Isabella herself withering "like a palm" (447) —a simile which reaffirms her attachment to this plant just as the previous description of her growing "like to a native lily" (366) beside Lorenzo's grave stated the relationship initially. Later, with just a hint of the same biological metaphor, she is said to be "drooping by the basil green" (458).

When the plant is taken from her, the metaphorical intensity decreases further. Figurative language flickers briefly in stanza 60 with "guerdon of their murder" and "blood upon their heads" (477, 480). The narrative is interrupted in stanza 61 by rather stilted invocations to personified Melancholy, Music, and Echo. But metaphorical language almost disappears in the last two stanzas. There is one bad mistake: Isabella mourning "with melodious chuckle in the strings / Of her lorn voice" (491–92). In the same stanza, her calling out to "the Pilgrim" (493) is very good, and ironic; the plain word is used, not the archaic and romantic one, *palmer,* which was used to describe Lorenzo in the second line of the poem. In the last stanza, with the possible exception of "story born / From mouth to mouth" (501–2), the figurative language flickers out altogether. The imagery sets.

Keats is less successful in his application of some of the other means of producing intensity; the shaping of imagery is good, but his attempts to use contrast and to give to his subject all possible associations are not as well managed. Structurally these result in the somewhat obtrusive digressions. The long digression, from stanzas 12 through 17, does two things which, theoretically, could have set off the main narration with greater intensity: it presents, with some vivid imagery the cruel contrast to the love affair which is the main subject of the narration, and it announces without subtlety the ethical posture of the narrator. Perhaps this digression is supposed to give the work some "moral" content along with its poetry, supposed to make it more "serious" and real than the fanciful ventures of *Endymion*. Perhaps Hazlitt's praise of Milton for adorning and dignifying his subjects with all possible associations, including the moral and intellectual, encouraged Keats to pound home the edifying rhetoric on greed and pride. The flamboyant rhetoric (stanza 16, for example), which resembles that of Fairfax's translation of Tasso's *Jerusalem Delivered*,[35] aggravates the intrusive character of this digression; and yet some hints of the careless pride of these brothers is perhaps necessary before we meet them, as preparation for the cruel action which forms part of the narrative.

The poet's apologies (19, 20, 49) do have some relevance to the theme, especially as a defense of the natural subject matter, but they also rather obtrusively interrupt the progress of the narration. In his invocations to Melancholy, Music, and Echo (stanzas 55, 56, and 61), Keats uses the convention of the digressive "complaint," and Finney and F. E. L. Priestley have suggested Chaucer as the most likely source.[36] The structural justification for the device is clear; these personified figures are asked to come and sing, because this is a sad story, and its heroine "Isabel is soon to be / Among the dead" (447). But these invocations are rather too obvious and artificial a means of intensifying the emotion here.

Even with these failures, however, the very attempt to incorporate some darker, threatening elements against which the lovers' happiness can be seen, and elements which then destroy that happiness, results in an intensity which is absent from *Endymion*. Later, in the narrative poetry of 1819, the intensity resulting from the conflict of malevolent forces and happy dreams ceases to be artificially contrived; it is incorporated into the structural media of character and action along with the carefully controlled progress of the imagery, a means of narrative shaping which Keats had already used successfully in *Isabella.*

Notes

1. Bernice Slote, *Keats and the Dramatic Principle* (Lincoln: University of Nebraska Press, 1958), p. 14.

2. Keats writes that poetry "should strike the Reader as a wording of his own highest thought, and appear almost a Remembrance" (*Letters of John Keats,* 1:238).

3. See for instance Finney, *Evolution of Keats's Poetry,* 1:237–45. Thorpe details the encounters of the poet and Hazlitt and traces Hazlitt's growing appreciation of Keats in "Keats and Hazlitt: A Record of Personal Relationship and Critical Estimate," *PMLA* 62 (June 1947): 487–502. Herschel M. Sikes observes verbal reminiscences of Hazlitt in Keats's work and locates their sources in "The Poetic Theory and Practice of Keats: The Record of a Debt to Hazlitt," *Philological Quarterly* 38 (October 1959):401–12.

4. *Examiner,* no. 399, pp. 541–42. The Round Table series as such began 1 January 1815 in the *Examiner.* The two-volume publication of 1817, however, includes several articles published even earlier in the *Examiner,* before the Round Table series began; Hazlitt's observations on Wordsworth's *Excursion,* for instance, appear in August 1814 and are included as part of *The Round Table* of 1817.

5. *Examiner,* no. 428 (26 May 1816), pp. 332–33.

6. *Letters of John Keats,* 1:166, 188; and *The Poetical Works and Other Writings of John Keats,* ed. Maurice Buxton Forman, the Hampstead edition, 8 vols. (New York: Charles Scribner's Sons, 1938–39), 5:230 (subsequent references to this edition are cited as Hampstead Keats).

7. The series, Lectures on the English Poets, was delivered during January and February 1818. See *The Complete Works of William Hazlitt,* ed. P. P. Howe, 21 vols. (London: J. M. Dent and Sons, 1930–34), 5:383. All references to Hazlitt's writings will be to this edition; hereafter cited as *Hazlitt Works.*

8. Letters of April and May contain specific references to Milton as Keats responds to this poet. See the letter to Reynolds, 27 April 1818 (*Letters of John Keats,* 1:274) and the letter to Reynolds, 3 May 1818 (ibid., 276). Keats had read *Paradise Lost* with Benjamin Bailey in September 1817, but the markings and annotations made by Keats and Charles W. Dilke in the winter, 1817–18, show the greatest evidence of Hazlitt's influence; see Finney, *Evolution of Keats's Poetry,* 1:336–40.

9. Rollins presents evidence that Keats read a manuscript of these lectures; see *Letters of John Keats,* 2:24–25, and p. 24 n. 2.

10. J. D. O'Hara, "Hazlitt and Romantic Criticism of the Fine Arts," *Journal of Aesthetics and Art Criticism* 27 (1968):80–82; Samuel S. Monk, *The Sublime* (Ann Arbor: University of Michigan Press, 1960), p. 171.

11. Monk, *The Sublime*, p. 121; John Margolis notes that both Hazlitt and Keats give the word *power* two meanings, using it sometimes to refer to an egocentric subjectivity, at other times to an objective intensity in a work of art; see "Keats's 'Men of Genius' and 'Men of Power'," *Texas Studies in Literature and Language* 11 (Winter 1970): 1333–47.

12. *Hazlitt Works*, 4:77.

13. Ibid., pp. 77–78.

14. Ibid., p. 79.

15. Ibid., pp. 79–80. My italics.

16. Ibid., p. 38.

17. Ibid., pp. 36–37.

18. Ibid., p. 163.

19. Keats copies this sonnet in a letter to his brothers, 24 January 1818 (*Letters of John Keats*, 1:214–15).

20. *Examiner*, no. 353, p. 636.

21. *Hazlitt Works*, 5:156.

22. Ibid., pp. 29, 35.

23. *Letters of John Keats*, 1: pp. 238–39.

24. David Perkins, *The Quest for Permanence* (Cambridge, Mass.: Harvard University Press, 1959), p. 205.

25. Hampstead Keats, 5:303–4.

26. Paul D. Sheats, "Stylistic Discipline in *The Fall of Hyperion*," *Keats-Shelley Journal* 17 (1968):76.

27. Jones, *John Keats's Dream of Truth*, pp. 111–12, 129, 226.

28. *Letters of John Keats*, 1:188–89.

29. Hampstead Keats, 5:230.

30. Ibid., p. 293.

31. For Keats's remarks on *Isabella* see *Letters of John Keats*, 2:162, 174. *Isabella* was probably begun shortly after Keats heard Hazlitt's suggestion, made in a lecture of 3 February 1818, that a translation of this tale of Boccaccio "could not fail to succeed in the present day." See *Hazlitt Works*, 5:82, and see de Selincourt, ed., *Poems of John Keats*, p. 460, for further discussion of the date of composition.

32. *Hazlitt Works*, 5:82.

33. Stillinger, *The Hoodwinking of Madeline*, pp. 36–41.

34. M. R. Ridley, *Keats' Craftsmanship* (Oxford: Clarendon Press, 1933), p. 23.

35. Bate observes that the excessive rhetorical repetitions in *Isabella* may have represented Keats's deliberate defiance of Hunt's strictures on repetition in his *Critique on Fairfax's Tasso;* Keats writes Haydon that Hunt has "damned" Italian tales. See *Letters of John Keats*, 1:252; Bate, *John Keats*, pp. 312–13.

36. Finney, *Evolution of Keats's Poetry*, 1:378. F. E. L. Priestley objects to Finney's exclusion of any but humorous instances of this device in Chaucer; Priestley cites more serious examples. See his "Keats and Chaucer," *Modern Language Quarterly* 5 (1944):442.

V

Lyric Narration: *The Eve of St. Agnes,* *La Belle Dame sans Merci,* and *Lamia*

In *Isabella,* Keats began to use imagery as a structuring element; in his later narrative poetry, he demonstrates the range and flexibility of this technique. The heavy ornamentation of *The Eve of St. Agnes* and *Lamia* effectively molds the action, just as the relatively sparse description in *La Belle Dame sans Merci* is subtly varied for the purposes of characterization and climax. Even when Keats's invention takes the fairy way, as it certainly does in *La Belle Dame sans Merci* and *Lamia,* it does not yield an unwieldy variety of fanciful subject matter. Instead, the poet uses imagery as a vehicle for sequence and climax; he increases the number of metaphors, or descriptive adjectives, during the narrative peaks of excitement, action, or perception. In *The Eve of St. Agnes, La Belle Dame sans Merci,* and *Lamia,* Keats demonstrates that he can write about time as well as eternity; he can build a sequence of events as well as create vividly pictured moments in response to an urn or a nightingale.

Earlier I called attention to the remarks of Abrams and Kroeber concerning the tendency of romantic poets to give their narratives lyric qualities. Lionel Stevenson, evidently observing the lyric elements in *The Eve of St. Agnes,* praises this poem as the "archetype" of romantic narration, because the "story is conveyed almost wholly through setting and mood." Stevenson describes further the liberties which Keats takes with our usual expectations regarding action and plot in a narrative context: "Regarded in terms of conventional narrative method, *The Eve of St. Agnes* flouts the basic rules. Suspense is built up meretriciously and then flagrantly disappointed. Angela's warnings lead us to expect a confrontation between Porphyro and his enemies, and the elaborate preparation of the supper seems like a foolhardy gesture that will ensure discovery." [1] Yet so well does Keats divert our attention to other things that we are not conscious of his unconventional handling of the narrative. Keats achieves suspense, but he achieves it by using lyric devices. A closer look at one of Stevenson's examples will clarify this point. Our attention, during Porphyro's preparation of the supper, for instance, is so caught up by the extended description of the delicious and exotic food, that we do not consider Porphyro's potentially dangerous situation. Keats does not ask us to consider it. An accomplished narrative poet now, he focuses our attention where he wants to focus it. Our suspense during this episode is Porphyro's suspense. He is not so much afraid of being discovered by the hostile Baron as he is of the possibility that Madeline may awake before his delicious banquet is prepared. Even before the hall door opens, letting in the noises of the reveling, he is "half-anguish'd," as he spreads a cloth on the table (255–56); he prays for a "Morphean amulet" (257) so that Madeline will not awake before all is ready. The suspense and excitement here are embodied in the elaborate preparations which he feels he must make before waking Madeline and which are so richly described: apple, quince, plum, gourd, jellies, "syrops, tinct with cinnamon; / Manna and dates," and "spiced dainties" (265–69). Suspense is achieved, but not by the manipulation of plot; it is achieved by the manipulation of imagery. In other words, a traditionally narrative (and dramatic) effect—suspense—is achieved by a traditionally lyric means: imagery.

This kind of imaginative transfer has resulted in the interesting hybrid, the "lyric narrative," which critics have begun to describe in a general way. The use of imagery as a structuring device is not entirely Keats's innovation, of course; it can be compared to Shakespeare's use of imagery as a means of emphasizing character and theme, as R. H. Fogle has observed.[2] Keats himself offers a description of the lyric narrative, a description which resembles Stevenson's remarks. Keats writes in 1819: "I wish to diffuse the colouring of St. Agnes eve throughout a Poem in which Character and Sentiment would be the figures to such drapery." [3] When the coloring is diffused throughout a poem, it can serve narrative as well as lyric purposes. Keats's awareness of the varied opportunities for using imagery can be seen also in his annotations near the beginning of *Troilus and Cressida.* His folio edition reads:

> *TROY.* I haue (as when the Sunne doth light a-scorne)
> Buried this sigh, in wrinkle of a smile:
>
> (1.1. 39)

Keats observes that "the Commentators have contrived to twist many beautiful passages into common places as they have done with respect to 'a scorn' which they have hocus pocus'd in[to] 'a storm' thereby destroying the depth of the simile—taking away all the surrounding Atmosphere of Imagery and leaving a bare and unapt picture." [4] As Keats's narrative poems show, his remarks here about the "surrounding Atmosphere of Imagery" have implications beyond the particular passage of Shakespeare; Keats controls the atmosphere of imagery in *The Eve of St. Agnes, La Belle Dame sans Merci,* and *Lamia* to indicate suspense and, sometimes, to suggest characterization. This gives the later poems, in contrast to *Endymion,* a quality of depth as well as a temporal dimension. In *Endymion* there is no background and no foreground. Endymion's thoughts, speech, and his own figure merge into descriptions equally thick; everything happens in a glittering middle-distance.

By directing the atmosphere of imagery toward narrative ends, Keats subtly, but very successfully, responds to the major challenge which has been facing poets since the nineteenth century, the challenge defined by Wasserman as the necessity to create a "cosmic system" as well as a poem. Keats does not quite create such a system in the three poems under consideration here, because he does not create a myth; he does, however, imply a context of value, a complete world of relationships and judgments, and such a context is what a myth implies. The famous imagery of these poems serves as an atmosphere, a surrounding and silent comment, providing the context of value which allows the reader to respond to, understand, and judge the characters in the foreground. In each of these poems, Keats does indeed create a world, and the lyric elements build that world as they build the poetic structure itself.

The world of *The Eve of St. Agnes* is beautifully and skillfully incorporated into the narrative form. The imagery is modulated, not only in relation to the emotional peaks of the narrative, but in relation to the characters whom this surrounding atmosphere reveals and complements. Perhaps the conflicting interpretations of *The Eve of St. Agnes*, and particularly of some of the characters in it, have resulted because readers gave insufficient attention to what Keats called the surrounding atmosphere of imagery. Jack Stillinger, for instance, argues that a frankly libidinous Porphyro "hoodwinks" the already "self-hoodwinked" Madeline, thus rescuing her from her religious-romantic fantasies into the realities of life; Stillinger cautions that the religious imagery, often applied to the lovers here, represents a "hyperbolic love language," just as it does in *Romeo and Juliet.* Stillinger does qualify his remarks by saying that he has portrayed Porphyro "in admittedly exaggerated fashion" as "peeping Tom and villainous seducer." [5] I think that the exaggeration rests largely in the suggestion that Madeline, but not Porphyro, is hoodwinked by fantasies of religion and romance. Porphyro, far from being a skeptical ravisher who brings the real world to Madeline's bedchamber, is himself hoodwinked by his devotion to her. The progressively vivid metaphors, and the increasing number of them, as Porphyro watches Madeline, provides a "drapery" of sensuous excitement and anticipation. Keats, in this poem, gives his romantic lovers a context of richness and fulfillment. The images do not undercut the romantic concerns of either Madeline or Porphyro, nor do they imply an atmosphere of chuckles and cynicism. Porphyro wants to enter Madeline's world, not destroy it. Probably Wasserman's interpretation of the poem, although rather metaphysical, remains truer to the context of imagery which shapes the action of *The Eve of St. Agnes;* he suggests that Madeline's beautiful dream, like Adam's, becomes truth, and Porphyro and she enter this truth briefly. [6]

The imagery shows a contoured progress which tends to

heighten and reinforce, rather than ironically undercut, the romantic ambitions of both the lovers. Twice the imagery rises in intensity—very quickly flaring and lapsing during the first three stanzas, more gradually rising again as Porphyro successfully completes his strategem, and then subsiding a little as the lovers escape into the storm.

The poem begins in a rather high key, the interrupted rhythms of the first five lines complementing the breathless, nearly painful intensity of the concrete pictures of the owl, the hare, and the numb fingers of the praying Beadsman; but the intensity manages to rise even higher when the simile of the Beadsman's "frosted breath, / Like pious incense from a censer old," combines prayer, frost, and death in an ecstatic image of a "death" that somehow manages to escape from itself. After this, the very relaxed tone of the last five words of the stanza is welcome: "while his prayer he saith" (1–9). One can hardly object here to the use of such a bland stage-direction word as "saith" to complete the rhyme and to end the stanza. The emotional rest is appropriate, even necessary, and is further sustained by the repetition of "His prayer he saith" at the beginning of the second stanza.

In stanza 1, only the three lines which describe the Beadsman's breath rise to metaphorical intensity. In stanza 2, however, the "sculptur'd dead" are given five lines and without any falling off of emotion in the last one, for it continues the ascent; the sculptured knights and ladies seem to "ache in icy hoods and mails" (14–18). In the third stanza the imagery level falls, probably at the fifth line: "The joys of all his life were said and sung." This metaphor is so common as to be scarcely metaphorical, and there are no metaphors in the remaining lines of the stanza, nor in the first three lines of stanza 4 which complete the Beadsman's exit.

With the "silver, snarling trumpets" (31), the imagery level rises again, but it does so more slowly this time, making brief bursts intermittently while the characters, Madeline, Porphyro, and then Angela, are introduced. First, we are asked to look at Madeline, to "turn, sole-thoughted" to her, rather than to the others among the "argent revelry":

> At length burst in the argent revelry,
> With plume, tiara, and all rich array,
> Numerous as shadows haunting fairily
> The brain, new stuff'd, in youth, with triumphs gay
> Of old romance. These let us wish away,
> And turn, sole-thoughted, to one Lady there. . . .
> [37–42]

The narrator pointedly dismisses the others, comparing them to "shadows," to fantasies of the mind. Madeline's character is described against a background of people who are compared to dreams. Then her brooding thoughts of St. Agnes's Eve are described in stanza 6; as Stillinger points out, Madeline is, like the Beadsman, absorbed in an "ascetic ritual," and the narrator calls the ritual which she anticipates a mere "whim" (55).[7] Heeding none of the men who approach her, she sighs "for Agnes' dreams, the sweetest of the year" (63). But notice that the opposition here is between dream and dream, not between dream and reality. Madeline is

> Hoodwink'd with faery fancy; all amort
> Save to St. Agnes and her lambs unshorn,
> And all the bliss to be before to-morrow morn.
> [70–72]

She is hoodwinked by a dream that results in bliss, and Porphyro wants to share this dream; she is "all amort" to other things, but the narrator gives no indication that she should be alive to anything else. Is she supposed to behave more like the other revelers, the "shadows"? Is she supposed to be a partisan in the feud? These alternatives would seem to deserve an "all amort" attitude; Madeline is an ascetic, in a sense, just as the Beadsman is. Both pray and fast. Both may be "hoodwinked" by their imaginations, but Porphyro is hoodwinked as well. The Baron and his guests are also hoodwinked, by their belief in the feud; more importantly, they are eventually hoodwinked by both Madeline and Porphyro, who escape, and leave them to their nightmares. The point is that Keats does not supply, in this poem, a context by which we can direct skepticism at Madeline and Porphyro; in *La Belle Dame sans Merci* and *Lamia*, on the other hand, he certainly does supply a context for skepticism.

Significantly, there is no piling up of involved metaphors during the stanzas which describe Madeline among the celebrating guests and which relate Porphyro's conversation with Angela. The dialogue of Porphyro and Angela is itself excited, breathless, suspenseful; but the "drapery" of imagery during this part of the poem is remarkably subdued. Once Madeline enters her chamber, however, the metaphors increase in number and vividness. The relatively restrained imagery when she is with the revelers reinforces the narrator's suggestion that she is all amort to them. She is not herself when she is in the context of the gay festivities, and appropriately the background imagery is less vivid. When she at last retires to her room, both her excitement and that of the hiding Porphyro are reinforced by some of the heaviest and most famous imagery in the poem.

Beginning with stanza 23, the imagery rises rapidly. Here Madeline, after helping Angela down the stairs, hurries into the room where Porphyro is hiding; the last four lines of the stanza are given to the development of a simile, describing her heart as a "tongueless nightingale" (204–7). The famous stanza 24 is given totally to an elaborate and vivid description of the casement window, a description whose very grammar is distinctly figurative—a casement "garlanded" and "diamonded," on which a "shielded scutcheon blush'd" (208–16). This is certainly an example of "grappling" with one's subject, of taking a double relish and repeating the blow.

The high point of the narrator's virtuosity in crowding and condensing metaphors occurs in stanza 27. Leigh Hunt, commenting on these lines in 1844, observes: "And how the imagery rises!" [8] The imagery has been steadily rising even before this stanza; now it is further intensified. Here there is almost one metaphor per line—seven in eight lines. The only line that is without metaphor is the second line. Most of these metaphors —as we might expect, considering the exigencies of space—are crammed into the past participle: "poppied warmth," a "soul fatigued away," "haven'd," and "Clasp'd like a missal" (235–43). Certainly in this stanza Keats is pursuing his subject to the utmost.

As Porphyro steps from his hiding place and begins to prepare the exotic feast, the heightened excitement of the imagery continues, although it no longer relies so much on metaphor as on the piling up of adjectives, "A cloth of woven crimson, gold, and jet," for instance, and the interruption by "The boisterous, midnight, festive clarion" (256–58). We have already observed that the extended description of the feast contributes much to the suspense during this part of the poem, and it does so largely without metaphor. The exotic delicacies are for the most part merely listed, although some are supplied with enriching adjectives or phrases: "candied apple," "lucent syrops, tinct with cinnamon," "spiced dainties" (265–69). One way or another, by metaphor or piles of nouns and adjectives, the context of heavy imagery continues to surround the lovers as the moment of their union arrives.

The stanza describing the consummation of the love (36) is suitably given a less excited imagery. Only two similes—the star and the rose's odor—are employed, and they fuse easily, instead of flashing quickly one after another:

> and like a throbbing star
> Seen mid the sapphire heaven's deep repose
> Into her dream he melted, as the rose
> Blendeth its odour with the violet. . . .

[316–24]

Keats makes the imagery do its utmost here, as he did while describing Porphyro's banquet, but now this utmost has to characterize a fulfilled desire, not one that struggles with excited anticipation.

After this, the imagery begins to fall—that is, the metaphors are briefer and fewer, and they extend for fewer lines at a time. The final stanza is without metaphor; the lovers, Angela, and the Beadsman are dismissed from the poem with simple statements, although Angela's death is described with realistic detail. The most vividly painful imagery, however, is used not to describe Angela's death, but the dreams of the well-reveled guests and of the feuding Baron; his troubled sleep evidently brings him suspicion of the "woe" (372) that has befallen him in the elopement of his daughter.

Because the formal elements of the poem so completely create its world of value, Keats no longer needs to address the forces of evil from the soapbox of a narrator's digression, as he did in *Isabella.* Instead, he weights the context of value in favor of some characters by carefully shaping the imagery which surrounds them. As we have seen, the imagery which forms the backdrop as Porphyro and Madeline meet implies the richness and fulfillment of their love; however, other figures in the poem have sometimes been misinterpreted because readers have failed to observe how Keats uses imagery for the purposes of characterization and evaluation. The Beadsman, for instance, has been too hastily assigned a negative role of simple contrast to the sensuous lovers. But the Beadsman, like Madeline in her chamber, is presented with a vivid "drapery" of sensuous images. The imagery surrounding him in the first three and one-half stanzas does not in any way encourage an attitude of cynicism or derision toward him. Wasserman affirms that the Beadsman is the antithesis of the revelers—all soul—while they are all flesh, and while Madeline and Porphyro achieve the fusion of these two opposites.[9] Bloom likewise sees the Beadsman as rigidly "spiritual" and life-denying: "His icy faith frames the passionate center of the poem. . . ."[10] Stillinger finds him "so engrossed in an ascetic ritual that he is sealed off from the joys of life."[11] And Stuart Sperry sees the Beadsman as a figure who, in this poem of "wish-fulfillment," participates in "a familiar form of sublimation that is introduced only to be rejected as ineffectual."[12] Perhaps these critics have not examined carefully what the poet wrote: Keats says of the Beadsman, "The joys of all his life were said and sung" (23). There may be some ambiguity here; the statement may mean that the Beadsman's very real, even physical, joys are simply past, or it may mean that he has never known any joys except those that were "said and sung" as part of ritual prayer. But this statement does not exist in isolation; its implication must be discovered from the clues given in the surrounding context of imagery and action. And the Beadsman's response to his vividly described surroundings and to "Music's golden tongue," (20) testify that he does indeed know what joy is. He is "Flatter'd to tears" (21) by the music; that is, he is charmed, beguiled, moved.[13] Perhaps, because he is old, he is especially moved, finding that the sound of youthful vigorous joy can still touch him. He recognizes its sound, because he has known it well. He weeps, not because he has never known joy, but because he certainly has known it and can recognize it. His faith is fervent, not "icy"; even the cold outward circumstances are transformed by simile into the fervor of a prayer: his "frosted breath" becomes "pious incense from a censer old" (6–7). Keats would not have employed such imagery if he had desired to present the man's faith as icy, ascetic, joyless. Perhaps his faith gave him joy, although there is no reason to suppose that he has never known sensuous, physical pleasure also. On the contrary, his empathetic response to his surroundings is a very sensuous one; his thinking that the carved knights and ladies "ache" reminds one, by the way, of Keats's own capacity to respond to, and imagine the feelings of, inanimate objects; Richard Woodhouse records of Keats: "He has affirmed that he can conceive of a billiard Ball that it may have a sense of delight from its own roundness, smoothness."[14] The Beadsman, like Keats himself, is keenly and imaginatively responsive. Nothing in these first few stanzas can support the assertion that he is "sealed off" from life's joys, or from its painful sorrows.

But what of his death? Isn't this a kind of judgment on the Beadsman's restricted values? The description of his death implies nothing cynical or ironic: "The Beadsman, after thousand aves told, / For aye unsought for slept among his ashes cold" (378). It is hardly his fault that he is old when the poem begins, or that "his deathbell" has already rung (22). Even during his last hours, this "patient, holy man" (10) stays awake to pray for his "soul's reprieve" and "for sinners' sake to grieve" (26–27). A more cynical interpretation could be given the altered version of the last few lines of the poem:

> Angela went off
> Twitch'd with the Palsy; and with face deform
> The Beadsman stiffen'd, 'twixt a sigh and laugh
> Ta'en sudden from his beads by one weak little cough.[15]

Perhaps Keats wanted to change his portrayal of the Beadsman and Angela, but merely changing the last lines would never have sufficed to portray the Beadsman as a grotesque figure; we still have the intense, heavy imagery of the first stanzas of the poem, and still the Beadsman's sensitive, even poetic, response to the carved figures surrounding him. The poem as it was first printed, in 1820—and as it continues to be printed—gives a consistent picture of the Beadsman; the attempted alterations in the last lines would have given an inconsistent picture, and would therefore have been a flaw in this work—unless, of course, the first stanzas *also* had been changed, in which case we would have had a quite different poem.

Perhaps it is the figure of Angela which has confused so many readers in their interpretation of the Beadsman's character; both figures are "religious," and a casual glance may carelessly put them both in the same pious perspective. Angela is, admittedly, silly and old, and perhaps she is grotesque. Her "fumbling pieties" have, however, been exaggerated.[16] She is not given the aura of imagery which shows the Beadsman's human, sensitive responses in a context of vivid beauty. She is talkative, pious, and nervous for Porphyro's safety, and then for Madeline's reputation. But "Angela the old" (375) is not merely, or stodgily, old, though she does typify the stereotype of one-half of the "generation gap"—her spoken ethic suggests one thing, but her actions in aiding Porphyro's stratagem manifest another. It is, in fact, her relationship to the other characters of the poem which accomplishes for her what the intense imagery accomplishes for the Beadsman; both of these structural maneuvers succeed in portraying the characters as responsive human beings, alert to joy, danger, and pain. Madeline, even though she is "all amort" to anyone else, still remembers Angela's need and helps her down the stairs. Apparently this act is a nightly habit, and so she does it even tonight, though she is "like a mission'd spirit, unaware" on this exceptional occasion (193). Our attitude toward Angela, a garrulous and somewhat comic figure, is qualified by Madeline's act here, which would not have been given so many lines if Keats had not wanted to encourage our sympathetic response to the nurse.

But she dies "palsy-twitch'd," even in the first version (376). Isn't that poetic justice for her having been a negative figure of foolish piety in the poem? Perhaps a reader's response to this line cannot escape a personal bias; perhaps the image of a "palsy-twitch'd" death is, in itself, grotesque to some, pathetic and pitiful to others. But this line, taken in the context of the rest of the poem and in the context of what we know about Angela, can hardly be seen as the grotesque punishment assigned by the poet to one of the poem's moral negatives. This manner of dying only confirms Angela's clear-sighted knowledge of herself; she knew she would die this way, knew she was a "feeble soul," a "poor, weak, palsy-stricken, churchyard thing" who might die this very night (154–56). She has already called herself everything the critics have. She knows she is feeble and old; she knows she will not die gracefully, and she does not. There is nothing in this fact, or in the characterization, imagery, or events of this narrative to assign either Angela or the Beadsman to the moral Ulro of the poem.

It is doubtful that Keats is here writing a poem whose moral or philosophical absolutes are as patent as some readers have assumed. He expresses dislike for poetry with such "a palpable design," [17] and works in *Isabella,* but with greater success in *The Eve of St. Agnes,* to make the contrasting elements serve the structural principle of intensity rather than a principle of ethics. Even the really "bad guys" of this poem—the Baron and his party of revelers—do not harshly jar its music; they are not here pointedly denounced from a narrator's rhetorical podium as are the greedy and proud brothers in the digressions of *Isabella.* The revelers here are dismissed by the narrator as "shadows" haunting "The brain, new stuff'd, in youth, with triumphs gay / Of old romance"; though the narrator suggests "These let us wish away" (39–41), he later descibes their ominous threat, taking Porphyro's point of view to do so in stanza 10. The Baron and his "bloodthirsty race" are characterized here more subtly than the brothers were in *Isabella,* through the eyes of other persons: Angela tells something of their nature (99–108) while she gives us at the same time a thorough picture of her own talkative, fearful one. And Porphyro makes use of the Baron's evil presence to secure Angela's aid by threatening to alert his "foeman's ears" to his trespass into the household (151–53).

The contrasting elements are managed poetically, narratively, structurally. The contrast is perhaps a three-way one— the revelers are opposed to the lovers and to the Beadsman and Angela, while the lovers, because of their youth which still renders them capable of fulfillment, are contrasted with the Beadsman and Angela who, although they have been young, are no longer physically able to grasp their happiness. There is no sharp cackle of judgment in the narrator's voice as he describes their deaths; only the pathetic reality is given. If there is anything grotesque in the poem, it is the "large coffin-worm" (374) which benightmares the Baron and his guests, and since no attempt has been made in the poem, through imagery or action, to align our sympathies with them, their grim dreams seem consistent with the feuds and folly of their waking lives. And even here we should use Keats's own qualified appraisal of the "grotesque": here, as in *Paradise Lost,* the "Magnitude of Contrast" is "softened by the contrast being ungrotesque to a degree," heaven and hell both moving "like music" throughout; or, as he wrote of the Italian engravings, "Grotesque to a curious pitch—yet still making up a fine whole."[18] *The Eve of St. Agnes* is likewise a fine whole, a complete world and a complete poem. The progress of imagery, its atmosphere around certain characters, and the structuring contrasts, all intensify the same music.

Keats creates another fine whole in his next narrative, *La Belle Dame sans Merci*. It is a fine whole, and yet it is famous for its inexplicables, its mystery. Keats has in fact built mystery into this poem. Although the wide range of possible derivations for the character of the lady, the "faery's child," contributes something to the mysteriousness of her fateful relationship to the knight, the reader's sense of her strangeness is largely the result of Keats's quite appropriate refusal to let us really see her. By contrast, we do gain a fairly clear perception of the distressed knight. His narration of his experience becomes particularly vivid as he relates his dream about the pallid faces and the gaping mouths of those who, like him, are enthralled by the lady. In other words, Keats is again utilizing imagery to subtly mold the characters of the poem and to reinforce the narrative peak of the action.

La Belle Dame sans Merci, probably written in April 1819,[19] shows the poet achieving "intensity," but doing so by using a more limited palette than he had allowed himself in *Isabella* and in *The Eve of St. Agnes.* In these earlier poems, Keats provided intensity by heavily loading some passages with metaphor or descriptive detail. The imagery of *La Belle Dame*, however, is very restrained, in keeping with the simplicity of the ballad tradition. Keats makes only spartan use of adjectives in the poem, and he avoids metaphor, except for "fever dew" (10), "death-pale" (38), and the figurative suggestion that there is a lily on the knight's brow and a fading rose on his cheeks (9, 11).

Keats adroitly adapts the bare and restrained qualities of ballad narration to his new axioms, which are essentially those of lyric poety. *La Balle Dame* is such a successful combination of lyric and narrative elements that Kroeber finds in this poem the completion of the lengthy process by which the ballad was transformed into a lyric poem.[20] The process, an ongoing concern of eighteenth-century ballad imitators, included the publication of *Lyrical Ballads*, "The Rime of the Ancient Mariner" being Coleridge's contribution to the new genre of the "literary ballad"; although Coleridge and Wordsworth were attempting to return to the simplicity of folk ballads, there was a tendency among other ballad writers to pad the stark proportions of the authentic ballad with heavy description, ornate syntax, and pointed moralizing.[21] *La Belle Dame sans Merci* clearly is an imitation of the older, simpler tradition. For the structural groundwork of this poem, Keats relies on the folk ballad conventions which usually included a simple diction, a minimal attempt at characterization, a tendency to focus on a single event, an implied fatalism, and lack of evaluative comment.[22]

The structure which Keats builds on this groundwork is essentially dramatic. In the first three stanzas, an unidentified observer, impressed by a knight's stricken appearance, questions him about the reasons for it; in the nine stanzas that follow the knight tells of the mysterious lady who sang to him, fed him, and then lulled him to sleep in her "elfin grot" where he dreamed of starved men whom she had evidently enthralled before him. Wasserman has thoroughly explored this dramatic structure, noting how the images of the first three stanzas gradually evolve into a symbolic coalescence of "nature" and "human values." Wasserman further describes the narrative patterns in the poem, suggesting that the knight is fulfilling the stages of the "pleasure thermometer" and progressing toward "essence" in his relationship with the strange lady; the knight's helplessness is reinforced by a consistent grammatical pattern in the first lines of stanzas 4 through 9, the knight acting in the first three of these, but the lady taking the initiative in the second group of three: "I met . . . I made . . . I set," giving way to "She found . . . She took . . . And there she lulled. . . ." [23]

Although I am not convinced that *La Belle Dame sans Merci* is yet another embodiment of the pleasure thermometer, I agree with this critic's identification of the dramatic and rhetorical elements at work in the poem's structure. I would add only that the structure is reinforced, with regard to the narrative elements of characterization and climax, by a subtle modulation of the imagery. The modulation is quite subtle, since Keats is to a great extent restricting himself to the simplicity of style which is characteristic of the ballad form. The traditional ballad does not usually supply abundant description; it does not give full characterization nor the full background of the events narrated. Keats builds on this convention, allowing it to emphasize the inexplicables of the tale. In particular, the fundamental mystery of the lady's character, which is a central element in the meaning of the poem, is a result, not so much of her eclectic literary ancestry, as it is a consequence of the way in which she is described; she is given only a thin, very rare, "atmosphere" of imagery. The knight is, relatively speaking, more fully characterized; we learn much more about him—and about the other men who have been similarly enthralled—than we are able to learn about the mysterious lady.

The observant questioner at the beginning of the poem provides a vivid and disturbing description of the knight. He is alone, pale, "haggard," "woe-begone" (1–8). His forehead is so pale that it resembles the whiteness of a lily, and the natural ruddiness of his cheeks is like a "fading rose" (9–12). He seems to be ill; his perspiration may imply emotional as well as physical stress, since the questioner says, "I see a lilly on thy brow, / with anguish moist and fever dew" (9–10). Since the final stanza nearly repeats the first one, our first impression of the knight, "alone and palely loitering," is reiterated and reinforced. Even though the knight has "explained"—has given us his story—the structure of the poem works against any sense of a progression toward enlightenment; as observers, we end where we began, with the picture of a pale knight, the withered sedge, and a lake where no birds sing.

Further, our final perception of the knight and his distress is heightened by the vision of the pale kings, princes, and warriors of his dream which he has just related. The imagery, although very subdued throughout the poem, becomes suddenly richer during the description of the dream. In *La Belle Dame sans Merci* the scanty atmosphere of imagery is almost entirely expressed by adjectives, rather than by metaphors. Usually a single adjective is laid next to an important noun: "fragrant zone" (18), "sweet moan" (20), "pacing steed" (21). We learn only this single quality about the zone, the moan, and the steed; also, the adjectives given to the respective nouns are not repeated for emphasis, although *sweet* does occur later in "relish sweet" (25). By contrast, the description of the men in the dream is fairly heavy:

> I saw pale kings and princes too,
>   Pale warriors, death-pale were they all;
> They cried—La Belle Dame sans Merci
>   Hath thee in thrall!
>
> I saw their starved lips in the gloam,
>   With horrid warning gaped wide,
> And I awoke and found me here,
>   On the cold hill's side.
>
> [37–44]

The lady's many victims are particularized—kings, princes, and warriors—and the adjective *pale* is emphatically repeated, approaching metaphor in the phrase, *death-pale*. The word occurs in adverbial form to describe the knight at the beginning and end of the poem: "Alone and palely loitering." In terms of the very restricted descriptions which Keats allowed himself in this short ballad, the occurrence of some form of the word *pale* five times contributes to the vivid perception we retain of the knight's distressed countenance; during the dream, the word recurs three times in two lines, and it is part of the picture which we are given of the knight as the poem begins and ends. Only the word *wild* is a contender, in terms of repetition; it is used three times to describe the lady's eyes (16, 31), and it occurs once in the phrase "honey wild" (26). These two prominent repetitions, *pale* and *wild,* may be significantly related to each other, since the knight's fascination with the lady, and especially her eyes (he closes them with "kisses four"), leads ultimately to his enthrallment, his fever, and his paleness.

The climax of the dream, however, is not the knight's vision of the paleness of the victims, or even their identification of the lady as "La Belle Dame sans Merci." The final, and most thoroughly portrayed horror, is the vision of the "starved lips." At this point, we are given two very rich, full lines, in contrast to the brief adjective-noun phrases elsewhere in the poem. We see the starved lips surrounded by a context of descriptive imagery: "starved lips in the gloam, / With horrid warning gaped wide" (41–42). The description of the lips has a function in this poem similar to the artificial rhetoric which Keats used in *Isabella* in order to pack in all "possible associations." The evaluative word *warning* is reinforced here by a context of vivid imagery; it becomes part of the narrative texture of the poem, rather than an extraneous, digressive comment. This climactic episode of the poem shows Keats masterfully at ease with the new narrative techniques which he had been developing.

In contrast to the striking details which allow us to see the knight, the description of the lady is quite sparse; we are never told very much about her. First, we learn that she appears "in the meads" (13). This brief hint of a landscape is probably significant, since meads, or meadows, are grasslands which often are found close to water, and the lady herself, as Bernice Slote suggests, may be a natural spirit associated with water; as naiad, she is not necessarily malevolent, but she destroys her lover simply because she is nonmortal and belongs to a different element.[24] Charles Patterson discusses Keats's knowledge of legends dealing with fairies, and he concludes that the lady of *La Belle Dame sans Merci* is "a nonmortal, daemonic creature of Celtic origins" who is neither good nor evil, being outside the human realm.[25] Keats could have read about such beautiful, and often destructive, female figures in several earlier works, including a medieval translation of Alain Chartier's poem *La Belle Dame sans Mercie,* Spenser's *Faerie Queene,* and several folk ballads which feature a fairy lady of mysterious character.[26] And of course some of the ambiguities of the lady's personality may be partly an expression of Keats's ambiguous love for Fanny Brawne.[27] Whatever the derivation of the fairy lady's personality in Keats's poem, her character is kept at a distance, and her mystery heightened, by the knight's failure, or refusal, to describe her specifically. In his description of her he is not as concrete and vivid as the initial questioner is in describing the knight himself.

The knight's first efforts to describe the woman tell us that she was "Full beautiful" (14). This bland generalization is the opposite of the concrete description which we expect from Keats. But the knight is speaking here, and he may not be representing Keats. The words, "Full beautiful," express the knight's interpretation of what he sees, not the visual details themselves. The knight then identifies the woman as a "faery's child" (14), and he seems to become more specific: "Her hair was long, her foot was light, / And her eyes were wild" (15–16). The musical linkage among the three adjectives is nice, *long* and *light* alliterating, and *wild* picking up the vowel of *light*. Appropriately, these lines, like the lady herself, sing and charm, but reveal little of her character or even of her appearance. The long hair does give us something visual, but the *light* foot is vague; presumably she is walking, and the knight is noticing that her feet scarcely press the grass. The adjective *wild* is, like "Full beautiful," an interpretation on the part of the knight; *wild* does not characterize the eye very specifically. The spareness of the description is of course quite consistent with the conventions of the folk ballad; what is significant here is that Keats, within the spareness of the convention, presents the knight to us more vividly than he does the lady. The comparative lack of characterization given to her tends to keep her at a distance from both the knight's evaluative efforts and from ours.

The description of her hair, foot, and eyes, can be usefully compared to Coleridge's description of "Life-in-Death" in "The Rime of the Ancient Mariner," another imitation of the ballad form: "*Her* lips were red, *her* looks were free / Her locks were yellow as gold" (190–91). Bloom has suggested that these lines

The Eve of St. Agnes, La Belle Dame, and *Lamia*

find a parallel in the two lines which describe the lady in Keats's poem.[28] The distinctions between the two descriptions are as interesting as the similarities. Coleridge's description gives us two conventional adjectives—*red* for lips, and *yellow* for hair —but these two bright colors do bring the face of Life-in-Death into grotesque prominence. Instead of the neutral *hair,* Life-in-Death has *locks,* a word which suggests heaviness and contour. The phrase "yellow as gold" lays yellow on yellow, reinforcing the vivid visual impression. In contrast, the fairy's child in Keats's poem seems to exist just on the edge of the visible spectrum. Her lack of physical characterization may represent her tangential relationship to the human sphere, a relationship implied by her nonmortal, fairy nature.

Her presence assumes a more specific character as the knight begins to act in relation to her. We see her adorned with a garland, with bracelets, and with the "fragrant zone" (17–18), because the knight constructs these things and gives them to her. Evidently these generous actions on the part of the knight result in the loving look and the sweet moan (19–20). We see her on the knight's steed, because he places her there. Since she was not singing earlier, the knight's action here seems to have been a symbolic gesture, necessary in order for her to "sing / A faery's song" (23–24). Certainly those critics are right who suggest that the knight initiates his own enthrallment.[29] His actions allow the mysterious woman to assume a personality as well as to trap him with this personality. His relationship with her gives her the characteristics which begin to define her identity.

Part of the enthrallment process, as is often the case in ballads, is the food which the lady gives to the knight. The food in this instance is rather specifically identified: "relish sweet, / And honey wild, and manna dew" (25–26). The descriptive attention given to the food is, in this poem of sparse descriptions, comparatively detailed. Although strange, the food seems real and convincing; ironically, it does not satisfy, but leads to the vision of the starved lips of the figures in the dream. The presence of specific and concrete imagery as the food is described perhaps reinforces the narrative relationship between this food and its effect, the starved lips, which are likewise described with relatively detailed and heavy imagery.

There is a subtle crescendo to the knight's involvement with the lady, and simultaneously an increasing willingness, on his part, to interpret her character. He provides her with gifts, puts her on the steed, listens exclusively to her song, and evidently accepts the exotic food she gives him; then, he ventures to interpret her "language strange": "And sure in language strange she said— / 'I love thee true' " (27–28). If the language is "strange," how can he be sure about what she says? Even if her fairy language is not utterly foreign and if its strangeness is merely a peculiarity of pronunciation, some barrier to communication might be expected between the human and the nonhuman.[30] The knight's dream, in fact, and his subsequent desolation suggest that he at some point certainly failed to understand the mysterious woman.

The knight becomes more and more deceived as he continues to interpret the lady's character. In a sense, he constructs her image to correspond with what he sees in her; she wears the adornments which he makes. When he interprets her "language strange," he is probably translating his hopes rather than her speech. The lady evidently plays the role of a stimulus to the knight's imagination; indeed, she may symobolize the imagination. As Newell Ford suggests, she may represent an instance of the "cheating" imagination.[31] But the knight cheats himself, since he may be seeing in the lady what is not there. The sustenance which he accepts from her leads only to starvation, and the fairy song which she sings is countered by his waking assertion that "no birds sing."

In *La Belle Dame sans Merci,* the essentially unadorned style is counterpointed by a somewhat fuller imagery at crucial points in the narrative. The fuller, more detailed, descriptions given to the knight's appearance and to his dream are associated with his self-deceiving attitude and with his tendency to see more than is there. Even though the lady's literary and mythological ancestry may imply that she is "unkind," it is the knight's false imagination which really causes his suffering. In this successful experiment with the ballad form, Keats carefully modulates the sparse imagery so that it reinforces narrative action and implies certain aspects of the characterization. The knight's physical and emotional distress is vividly presented, while the mysterious fairy lady's presence is given only the lightest sketch. She remains on the fringes of mortal perception, and for this reason she is a fascinating but potentially dangerous stimulus to the human imagination.

Again, in *Lamia*, Keats places an ambiguous female personality at the center of the poem's meaning. While he had implied the personality of a mysterious woman, in *La Belle Dame sans Merci*, by using a very restrained style of description, in *Lamia* he achieves a similar result but by a very different means. Lamia is a more active figure than the fairy in the earlier poem; Lamia's magical ability to create illusion is often represented by heavy and extended descriptions. While the main structuring element in *Lamia* is a repetitive design similar to that used in *Endymion*, the imagery in the later poem shows a "progress" much like that in *The Eve of St. Agnes*. The imagery tends to break suddenly into brilliance, often a prolonged brilliance, when Lamia is present; the surrounding atmosphere of imagery defines her character's vivid, though illusory and dangerous, richness. The double, repetitive structure and the imagery are closely associated with her character, and it may be this association which has caused some readers to find flaws in the poem's structure as well as in its "theme," if a poem with a main character like Lamia can be said to have one theme.

Keats so well integrates structure and character in *Lamia* that the poem has been criticized for its obviously double form; the form's two parallel yet contrasting parts seem to yield a broken narrative and hence a defective work. But there is more than one sort of doubleness in this poem whose main figure is a beautiful, probably deceitful, and certainly uncategorizable woman; the repetitive device is used internally to suggest the dubious quality of Lamia's character. This poem is a little like Lamia's banquet room, full of "mirror'd walls" (2. 182) whose reflections subtly complicate the apparently dual construction of simple parallel-and-contrast.

Apart from this major criticism, the lesser objections and misgivings have for the most part been allayed. Colvin's "bewilderment" about the "effect intended to be made on our imaginative sympathies" [32] has been explained: some such bewilderment is to be expected from the very manner in which the characters are presented; the reader cannot expect his sympathies to be directed to any one of them as a secure ethical positive or negative, since they are presented "objectively" or "dramatically." The best discussion of Keats's dramatic method in *Lamia*, a poem which he interrupted in order to collaborate with Charles Brown on their drama, *Otho the Great*, is given by Slote, who aptly describes the poet's relationship to *Lamia:* "The personal position of Keats in the poem is that of producer."[33] The good dramatist does not assign easy ethical labels to his characters. On the contrary, he utilizes every means, including the very structure of the work itself, to let the characters develop into whatever they are; and Lamia *is* "bewildering."

An apparent shift of tone between part 1 and part 2 of *Lamia* has sometimes been blamed for the reader's poorly guided and therefore confused response to Lamia's character. According to Finney, the second part shows an attempt to imitate the sportive, satiric style of Byron, while the first part is symbolic, Lamia representing the poetic imagination and Lycius the poet.[34] Some shift in tone might be expected, since Keats worked on *Otho the Great* for several weeks between the two parts of *Lamia*,[35] but not every reader finds this supposed change of tone. Georgia Dunbar argues that the change is merely one of degree, not of kind, shifting from gentle mockery to satire and sarcasm.[36] Warren Stevenson and David Perkins find a consistent tone of irony throughout the poem; Perkins sees the "ironic detachment," which Keats may have borrowed from Dryden, present in the "quick, college-cheer movement" of the lines used to describe Lamia:

> Striped like a zebra, freckled like a pard,
> Eyed like a peacock, and all crimson barr'd.
>
> [1.49–50]

The rhythm of these lines, observes Perkins, plus "the incongruity of the menagerie and the kaleidoscope of color all define an attitude toward her."[37] And this attitude, which keeps our moral sympathies in bewilderment and which the imagery and rhythm enforce, is also supported by the structure of the poem itself, especially in the deviously duplicated presentation of some of its events.

The most comprehensive parallel structure in the poem is of course the implied comparison of Hermes' successful love affair with Lycius's unsuccessful one. Hermes, like Lycius, tries to get away with something; he succeeds, but Lycius does not. The crafty god is "bent warm on amorous theft" and is trying to avoid Jove; he has sneaked off to Crete "to escape the sight / Of his great summoner" (1. 7–12). Similarly, Lycius, while he and Lamia approach their mysterious home in Corinth, tries to avoid the eyes of Apollonius (1. 373–77). Both the god and the man love a supernatural being who tends to faint and fade. When Hermes approached the nymph,

> she, like a moon in wane,
> Faded before him, cower'd, nor could restrain
> Her fearful sobs, self-folding like a flower
> That faints into itself at evening hour.
>
> [1. 136–39]

When Lamia threatens to fulfill her lover's fears that she will fade away (1. 260–87), it is all done in order to entangle him more securely. Hermes, with his immortal warmth, takes the chilled hand of the nymph and embraces her (1. 140–43); but when Lycius presses the pale hand of Lamia as Apollonius looks at her, this merely mortal lover cannot keep the "aching ghost" from vanishing, and his arms are "empty of delight" as he dies (2. 294, 307–08). Hermes' nymph may be a "dream," but "Real are the dreams of Gods" (1. 126–27), and the god and his dream fly off into a real forest—into "the green-recessed woods" (1. 144). Lamia, on the other hand, is not a "real" dream, or at least not a real one when her relationship with Lycius is to be made manifest by a public marriage celebration, for she fades under the eye of Apollonius (2. 245–308); and the wedding feast takes place in a banquet room whose carved walls, "mimicking a glade" (2. 125), make a futile attempt to imitate the living forest into which Hermes disappeared with his nymph.

These parallel features, with their significant variations in the two juxtaposed stories, do indeed cohere in a thematic relationship: the dreams of the gods are real, while those of men are not. This is not the whole theme, however, and because of their failure to recognize the fact, many critics still find the structural juxtaposition unsatisfactory. The "prefatory episode," says Perkins, has no "organic connection with the story that follows"; and Wasserman objects that the story of Hermes and the nymph is irrelevant to the subsequent action.[38] But Keats not only relates the two episodes thematically, he uses the first one to provide a context by which the reader can observe and judge Lamia's character before its more elaborate manifestation in relation to Lycius and Apollonius begins to blur one's ability to judge it.

The relationship of the two episodes to each other is not as important as their relationship to the mysterious character, Lamia, whose name gives the poem its title; the poem is about her, not Lycius. She moves easily in the world of gods and in the world of men. The dreams of gods are real, those of men unreal, and those of Lamia partake of both qualities. Appropriately, then, we see her in both worlds, and we see her dreaming in both of them.

In the first few lines of the poem, the poet himself describes the descent of Hermes to earth:

> The ever-smitten Hermes empty left
> His golden throne, bent warm on amorous theft:
> From high Olympus had he stolen light,
> On this side of Jove's clouds, to escape the sight
> Of his great summoner, and made retreat
> Into a forest on the shores of Crete.
>
> [1. 7–12]

Lamia has observed these same events—in a "splendid dream":

> 'I saw thee sitting, on a throne of gold,
> 'Among the Gods, upon Olympus old,
> 'The only sad one; for thou didst not hear
> 'The soft, lute-finger'd Muses chaunting clear,
> 'Nor even Apollo when he sang alone,
> 'Deaf to his throbbing throat's long, long melodious moan.
> 'I dreamt I saw thee, robed in purple flakes,
> 'Break amorous through the clouds, as morning breaks,
> 'And, swiftly as a bright Phoebean dart,
> 'Strike for the Cretan isle; and here thou art!
> 'Too gentle Hermes, hast thou found the maid?'
>
> [1. 69–80]

The Eve of St. Agnes, La Belle Dame, and Lamia

Why are we given two versions—one from the poet and one from the mouth of an ambiguously beautiful serpent-woman? And why are the two accounts so different? The first, though in an indulgent, light tone, emphasizes Hermes' stealth and it hints of his shirking greater responsibilities: theft, stolen, escaped, the summoner. Lamia's account, her "dream," ignores this aspect altogether, and it adds a glittering atmosphere of imagery which is very flattering to Hermes. Instead of dismissing this latest amorous interest as typical of an "ever-smitten" god, Lamia glamorizes it with all the trimmings of melancholy love-sickness. The only item that is simple and the same in each account is the mention of the golden throne of the god. Lamia is a "smooth-lipp'd serpent," as Hermes immediately perceives (1. 83), and he responds to her flattery by recognizing that she wants something from him—"whatever bliss thou canst devise" (1. 85)—and that he will get his nymph in exchange. Lamia's dream here, or perhaps merely her *account* of it, corresponds only partially to the "facts" as the poet narrated them. Either her dreams do not reveal—even to her—the true circumstances of an event, or she disguises these circumstances, when she relates the dream, in order to achieve her own ends.

Before the second of the parallel episodes of this poem, we are given a rather lengthy account of Lamia's ability to dream "Of all she list" (1. 204). She dreams what she wants to dream, whether of gods or men, and she can "blend" her dream with the feasts and riots of men:

> And once, while among mortals dreaming thus,
> She saw the young Corinthian Lycius
> Charioting foremost in the envious race,
> Like a young Jove with calm uneager face,
> And fell into a swooning love of him.
>
> [1. 215–19]

We know that this dream of Lamia's is true, because it is proved so by the subsequent development and unhappy termination of her affair with Lycius. She sees in her dream that he is proud and that he considers himself to be in competition with his friends. She sees also that he is calm and uneager—characteristics which he has doubtless learned from his "trusty guide," (1.

375) Apollonius. This is the poet's account of what Lamia dreamed; it is not Lamia's own account.

When she herself relates to Lycius her first sight of him, there is no correspondence at all to her first sight of him as it was related by the narrator who said that she saw him, in her dream, at a race. She says she had lived content in Corinth

> Till she saw him, as once she pass'd him by,
> Where 'gainst a column he leant thoughtfully
> At Venus' temple porch, 'mid baskets heap'd
> Of amorous herbs and flowers, newly reap'd
> Late on that eve, as 'twas the night before
> The Adonian feast.
>
> [1. 315–20]

It is extremely doubtful, from what we know, or later learn, of Lycius—his love of masculine, competitive sport, and his studies under Apollonius—that he was ever lolling against a column of the temple of Venus. And even if this unlikely event is true, Lamia is lying when she says that she was a woman living in Corinth; if she saw him at Venus's temple, it was in one of her "dreams" as a serpent. We do know that just before Lycius met Lamia, he had offered a sacrifice to Jove, and there are some hints that this had to do with a desire for love, although his sacrifice might have been for reasons utterly unconnected with love. We are told: "Jove heard his vows, and better'd his desire" (1. 229). Does this mean that Lycius had just begun to have some interest in love and that Jove had now increased this interest? Or does it mean that his prayers here had nothing to do with love at all, but that Jove decided to turn Lycius's thoughts in this direction anyway? The implication is not clear. What is clear is that Lycius's interest in love is new and untypical of him and hence leaves him ripe for a foolish fall; it is also clear that Lamia is deceiving him in her account of their first meeting.

After encountering Lamia on the road to Corinth, Lycius is in a trance. He wakes from one trance into another as Lamia sings (1. 296–97); he is "blinded" by her "spell" that makes the distance to Corinth seem short; and just before he sinks completely into his dream, he perceives that he is not living in reality, for he recognizes Apollonius, who "seems / The ghost of folly haunting my sweet dreams" (1. 376–77). Lycius is now dreaming, and his dream proves ultimately unreal; it grows pale and finally vanishes as do the dreams of men.

But what of Lamia's dream—her dream of happiness with Lycius? It was not as real as the dreams of the gods, but not as unreal as those of men. Hermes was not deceived by his dream of the nymph—"Real are the dreams of gods"; Lycius was deceived by Lamia, the "foul dream"; and Lamia, like the gods, was not really deceived by her dreams—she knew that Lycius's character was proud, ambitious of acclaim. She also knew he was a mortal and that this affair, unlike that of Hermes and the nymph, could not possibly last forever. And yet she "fell into a swooning love of him"—fell in love, as though she were as helpless in this emotion as the human being Lycius is. She exists between the worlds of gods and men, and the parallel structure of the poem, with its contrasting yet similar episodes, shows her in relation to both worlds, dreaming in both, though deceiving others only in the world of men. Both worlds must therefore be seen, not only for the thematic contrast of the mortal and immortal realms, but in order that the poem may present an adequate picture of Lamia's mysterious character.

Her strange, doubtful, bizarre, even dangerous, character is also emphasized by the aura of imagery which surrounds her, especially when she is alone or when she magically controls her environment. Neither Lycius nor Apollonius is given a similarly vivid "surrounding atmosphere." The rich descriptive passages of this poem have already a well-established reputation. But these passages do not occur in isolation; they are part of a narrative poem, and some of their brilliance depends, I think, on the fact that they are part of the background "drapery" for Lamia's appearances and that they follow passages of rather subdued writing. Bush feels that *Lamia* is "too much of a brilliant piece of tapestry." [39] Perhaps the standard of "too much" depends somewhat on individual taste; what I wish briefly to show is that Keats's tapestry in this poem is a weave of bright colors which includes some rather neutral ones as well.

Our first view of Lamia is the one Hermes has; she is a snake, yet beautiful in a strange sort of way:

> She was a gordian shape of dazzling hue,
> Vermilion-spotted, golden, green, and blue;
> Striped like a zebra, freckled like a pard,
> Eyed like a peacock, and all crimson barr'd;
> And full of silver moons, that, as she breathed,
> Dissolv'd, or brighter shone, or interwreathed
> Their lustres with the gloomier tapestries.
>
> [1.47–53]

The images and the rhythm of this descriptive passage produce, as we earlier observed, an uncertain, cautionary, perhaps amused response on the part of the reader. There follow a hundred lines of dialogue, of political flattery, which do not develop any sustained descriptions of intensity equal to the first passage describing Lamia. Then, when Lamia is "Left to herself," her metamorphosis occurs in a passage as vivid, as odd, and as uncomfortable as the former one:

> Her mouth foam'd, and the grass, therewith besprent,
> Wither'd at dew so sweet and virulent;
> Her eyes in torture fix'd, and anguish drear,
> Hot, glaz'd, and wide, with lid-lashes all sear,
> Flash'd phosphor and sharp sparks, without one cooling tear.
>
> [1. 148–52]

The violent transformation continues until nothing "but pain and ugliness" remain (1. 164); finally, there is nothing left but "her new voice luting soft" (1. 167). Early in this narrative, we begin to realize that passages of the most intense description accompany the ambiguously beautiful character, Lamia. In *The Eve of St. Agnes* Keats shaped our responses to Porphyro, Madeline, and the Beadsman by giving them a bejewelled background of imagery; in *Lamia* a similar poetic strategy is at work, although the emotional tone is different. In *Lamia* the orchestra plays most loudly, the stage-lighting is most spectacular, when Lamia enters, exits, or acts in a manner that typifies her magical ambiguity.

When Lamia meets Lycius, their conversation is a texture of rationalizations, flattery, and lovers' pleas of helplessness. We are given no vivid detailing of the beauty which captures Lycius: "soon his eyes had drunk her beauty up" (1. 251). We do not have the opportunity here to see what he sees. Perhaps the significance of this passage of low-key narration is that it allows us to maintain a distance from Lamia which Lycius cannot maintain. Also, the subdued descriptive luster of their meeting appropriately corresponds to Lamia's efforts to seem like a real, earthly woman, not a goddess.

As the couple enter Corinth, the imagery rises abruptly (1. 350 ff), and it becomes especially brilliant as they arrive at Lamia's mysterious, impressive dwelling:

> Sounds Aeolian
> Breath'd from the hinges, as the ample span
> Of the wide doors disclos'd a place unknown
> Some time to any, but those two alone,
> And a few Persian mutes, who that same year
> Were seen about the markets: none knew where
> They could inhabit; the most curious
> Were foil'd, who watch'd to trace them to their house.
>
> [1. 386–93]

And by now we have come to associate such descriptive intensity with the magical and with Lamia herself. The atmosphere of imagery surrounds her character with mystery and ambiguity. Apollonius, by contrast, is never given this sort of backdrop. As he encounters Lamia and Lycius, he is barely, but effectively, sketched in:

> one came near
> With curl'd gray beard, sharp eyes, and smooth bald crown,
> Slow-stepp'd, and robed in philosophic gown.
>
> [1. 363–65]

The very general, but very appropriate phrase, "philosophic gown," shows an almost neoclassic austerity. When he needs to be, Keats can be nonconcrete, nonromantic. In this poem he allocates the vividness to Lamia, the spare generality to Apollonius. In other words, he uses the imagery for purposes of characterization.

The argument of Lycius and Lamia which fills the first hundred lines of part 2 contrasts sharply with the suddenly dazzling description of the banquet hall when Lamia is "left alone" to arrange and probably create it (2. 106–45). Near the beginning of this long description, the narrator makes a point of associating Lamia's fairy handiwork with doubtful architectural substance:

> A haunting music, sole perhaps and lone
> Supportress of the faery-roof, made moan
> Throughout, as fearful the whole charm might fade.
>
> [2. 122–24]

What Lamia does in dressing the banquet hall, Keats does with the imagery of the entire poem; the brilliant atmosphere, when it is most brilliant, hovers around Lamia's character and implies the presence of magical enchantment.

The banquet room continues to glow with vivid details while the guests enter (2. 173–98) and while they drink and talk (2. 199–200). The narrator's voice enters to assign symbolic wreaths to the major characters and to remark: "Do not all charms fly / At the mere touch of cold philosophy (2. 229–30)?" And by this time the poem's imagery has already begun to fall, to "set"; as Apollonius's eye wilts Lamia, the music in the hall ceases, and the myrtle sickens "in a thousand wreaths" (2. 263–64). The imagery completes its progress as Lamia fades, its brilliance having been all along closely linked to her doubtful character. In this lyric narrative, Keats has carefully worked the imagery into the weave of the total poetic texture.

In *Lamia*, in *The Eve of St. Agnes*, and in *La Belle Dame sans Merci*, Keats writes excellent narrative poetry, building a coherent structure which depends mainly on a carefully controlled background of imagery. In *The Eve of St. Agnes* the imagery implies characterization and linear climax; in *La Belle Dame sans Merci*, the restrained imagery of the ballad convention is carefully modulated to distinguish the suffering mortal and the mysterious lady; and the magical atmosphere of *Lamia* combines with a double structure to portray the complex ambiguities of the main character. Imagery supplies a subtly evaluative context in all three poems which helps to determine our emotional and intellectual response to the characters and to their actions. In these lyric narratives Keats very successfully builds, by means of the structuring elements themselves, a complete whole, a complete world.

The Eve of St. Agnes, La Belle Dame, and Lamia

Notes

1. Lionel Stevenson, "The Mystique of Romantic Narrative Poetry," in *Romantic and Victorian*, ed. W. Paul Elledge and Richard L. Hoffman (Cranbury, N.J.: Fairleigh Dickinson University Press, 1971), pp. 35–38; and see above, pp. 4–5.
2. Richard Harter Fogle, *The Imagery of Keats and Shelley* (Chapel Hill: University of North Carolina Press, 1949), p. 21.
3. See the letter to Taylor, 17 November 1819 (*Letters of John Keats*, 2:234).
4. The passage from *Troilus and Cressida* along with Keats's annotation on it is reproduced by Caroline Spurgeon, *Keats's Shakespeare* (London: Oxford University Press, 1928), p. 149.
5. Stillinger, *The Hoodwinking of Madeline*, pp. 67, 72–73, 82.
6. Earl Wasserman, *The Finer Tone: Keats' Major Poems* (Baltimore: Johns Hopkins Press, 1967), pp. 101–12.
7. Stillinger, *The Hoodwinking of Madeline*, p. 85.
8. Hunt, ed., *Imagination and Fancy*, pp. 336–37.
9. Wasserman, *The Finer Tone*, pp. 127–30.
10. Bloom, *The Visionary Company*, pp. 379–80.
11. Stillinger, *The Hoodwinking of Madeline*, p. 84.
12. Sperry, *Keats the Poet*, p. 206.
13. Compare Hunt's response to *flattered;* after some observations on the psychology of self-pity, Hunt proceeds to a characterization of the Beadsman—"a painstaking pilgrim, aged, patient, and humble"—which is fairly accurate, although not complete and not related to the surrounding imagery. See Hunt, ed., *Imagination and Fancy*, pp. 332–33. *The Oxford English Dictionary*, quoting line 21, interprets the contemporary meaning of *to flatter* as "To beguile, charm away (sorrow, etc.); also to beguile, charm *to* (tears)"; see vol. 4, item 6.
14. *Letters of John Keats*, 1: 389.
15. Keats altered the last four lines of *The Eve of St. Agnes* in September 1819; see Garrod, ed., *Poetical Works*, p. 256.
16. This is Bloom's phrase; see *The Visionary Company*, p. 380.
17. See the letter to Reynolds, 3 February 1818 (*Letters of John Keats*, 1:224): "We hate poetry that has a palpable design upon us—and if we do not agree, seems to put its hand in its breeches pocket. Poetry should be great & unobtrusive, a thing which enters into one's soul, and does not startle it or amaze it with itself but with its subject." The context of these remarks indicates that Keats objects to any poet —and his example is Wordsworth—who tries to force a particular philosophical position on the reader; no one wants "to be bullied into a certain Philosophy" (ibid. p. 223).
18. See entry for 31 December 1818 in the journal letter to the George Keatses (*Letters of John Keats*, 2:19). For a reproduction of one of these engravings see Gittings, *John Keats*, plates following p. 304.

19. Keats wrote the poem into a letter in April 1819; see *Letters of John Keats,* 2:95–96.
20. Kroeber, *Romantic Narrative Art,* pp. 41–45.
21. Ibid., pp. 12–47. Kroeber briefly compares *La Belle Dame sans Merci* with Chatterton's *Bristowe Tragedie,* an ornate ballad imitation; see pp. 36–38.
22. Kroeber, *Romantic Narrative Art,* pp. 27–38. For an extensive discussion of the authentic ballad of oral tradition, see Gordon Hall Gerould, *The Ballad of Tradition* (Oxford: Clarendon Press, 1932), pp. 1–14, 84–130. Albert B. Friedman notes the intrusion, in *La Belle Dame sans Merci,* of some elements of the metrical romances; see *The Ballad Revival* (Chicago: University of Chicago Press, 1961), pp. 294–300. Finney argues that Keats stays close to the simplicity of the ballad, as far as style is concerned; see *Evolution of Keats's Poetry,* 2:598–99.
23. Wasserman, *The Finer Tone,* pp. 65–83.
24. Bernice Slote, "La Belle Dame as Naiad," *Journal of English and Germanic Philology* 60 (January 1961): 22–30.
25. Charles I. Patterson, Jr., *The Daemonic in the Poetry of John Keats* (Urbana: University of Illinois Press, 1970), pp. 1–21, 138.
26. According to Leigh Hunt, the title of Keats's ballad is taken from the poem of the same name by Alain Chartier; see headnote to *La Belle Dame sans Merci* in Garrod, ed., *Poetical Works,* p. 441. For discussion of some specific sources for the lady's character, see Finney, *Evolution of Keats's Poetry,* 2:595–98, and Wasserman, who considers the relationship of Keats's poem to the ballad, "Thomas Rhymer"; see *The Finer Tone,* pp. 68–70. Bernice Slote discusses the popularity of Scottish ballads and of Scottish literature generally during 1818 and 1819; she points to some features of *La Belle Dame sans Merci* that may have been influenced by the contemporary enthusiasm. See her "The Climate of Keats's 'La Belle Dame sans Merci,'" *Modern Language Quarterly* 21 (1960): 195–207.
27. See for instance Finney, *Evolution of Keats's Poetry,* 2:593, and Edward Bostetter, *The Romantic Ventriloquists* (Seattle: University of Washington Press, 1963), p. 160.
28. Bloom, *The Visionary Company,* p. 386; and see "The Rime of the Ancient Mariner" from Coleridge's *Poetical Works* (1834) in *The Annotated Ancient Mariner,* ed. Martin Gardner (New York: Clarkson N. Potter, 1965), p. 65.
29. Wasserman, *The Finer Tone,* pp. 78–80. Patterson agrees with Wasserman and emphasizes the point; see *The Daemonic in the Poetry of John Keats,* pp. 141–42.
30. Jane R. Cohen has also pointed out the illogic of the knight's interpretation of the "language strange," but she sees this as simply another inconsistency in a hastily composed poem which Keats wrote in an offhand, humorous mood. See "Keats's Humor in 'La Belle Dame sans Merci,'" *Keats-Shelley Journal* 17 (1968): 10–13.

31. Newell Ford, *The Prefigurative Imagination of John Keats* (Hamden, Conn: Archon Books, 1966), p. 141.

32. Colvin, *John Keats,* p. 408.

33. Slote, *Keats and the Dramatic Principle,* p. 140.

34. Finney, *Evolution of Keats's Poetry,* 2:695–98.

35. See the letter to J. H. Reynolds, 11 July 1819, where Keats says that he has finished one act of *Otho the Great* and has "in the interval of beginning the 2d" proceeded with *Lamia,* finishing the first part; and the letter to Taylor, 5 September 1819, where the poet says that since finishing *Otho,* he has finished *Lamia* (*Letters of John Keats,* 2:128, 157).

36. Georgia S. Dunbar, "The Significance of Humor in 'Lamia'," *Keats-Shelley Journal* 8 (Winter 1959): 21.

37. Warren Stevenson, "*Lamia:* A Stab at the Gordian Knot," *Studies in Romanticism* 11 (1972): 241–52; Perkins, *Quest for Permanence,* p. 267.

38. Perkins, *Quest for Permanence,* p. 265; Wasserman, *The Finer Tone,* p. 158. While Wasserman sees the introductory episode as irrelevant to the later action, he does admit a thematic connection with which I basically agree: in the world of the gods love prospers eternally, but in the human world it is frustrated. See pp. 161–62. Donald H. Reiman suggests that there is mutability even in the realm of the gods, since they are constructed merely by human imagination; see "Keats and the Humanistic Paradox: Mythological History in *Lamia,*" *Studies in English Literature, 1500–1900* 11 (Autumn 1971): 659–69.

39. Bush, *Mythology and the Romantic Tradition,* p. 110.

VI

Fragmentary Visions: *The Eve of St. Mark* and the Hyperion Experiment

Among the most successful of Keats's early experiments with structure were the poems in which visions reiterated and varied the images received from a landscape. Keats again turns to the concept of a vision in two of his later poems: *The Eve of St. Mark*, and the Hyperion poem which resulted in the two fragments, *Hyperion* and *The Fall of Hyperion*. Certain elements of the bardic trance are present in *The Fall of Hyperion*, and a twofold structure, similar to that of the bardic trance, governs some sections of *Hyperion*. But Keats also brings to the Hyperion attempt several new concepts which contribute to the form of his projected "epic." He developed, from some suggestions of Hazlitt, a concept of the epic as a poem of static, monumental objects and characters, and he tried to compose an epic along these lines in *Hyperion;* he evidently perceived that such objects and characters more appropriately belonged to a world of vision in which they could appear as grand and memorable images in the poet's dream—thus Moneta presents them in *The Fall of Hyperion*. Structure, then, in the two Hyperion fragments, is the result of Keats's imaginative experimentation with several forms: the bardic trance, epic, and a dream-vision structure which he probably borrowed from Chaucer. Along with *The Fall of Hyperion, The Eve of St. Mark* incorporates several elements of the Chaucerian dream-vision; for this reason, a brief discussion of Chaucer's dream poems and of *The Eve of St. Mark* will provide a useful introduction to an examination of the Hyperion experiment.

Fragmentary Visions: *The Eve of St. Mark*

The Eve of St. Mark is at first glance a poem very similar to *The Eve of St. Agnes;* the titles of the poems are much alike, and both are rich in descriptive imagery. Perhaps *The Eve of St. Mark* is the beginning of another lyric narrative in which the atmosphere of imagery was to have been an important element in the structuring of action and character. As another element in the structure, Keats may have been considering the sharply dichotomized form of the Chaucerian dream-vision. The character Bertha reappears, or at least the same name appears again, in the fragmentary fantasy, "The Cap and Bells"; if the two fragments are related, some of the fantasy which was originally to have belonged to Bertha's dream—assuming that she will fall asleep while reading—may have been later recast in "The Cap and Bells."

In *The Eve of St. Mark*, which was most likely written in February 1819, Keats includes some lines which he says are a deliberate "imitation of the Authors in Chaucer's time." [1] In March, as he writes to America, he refers to the two volumes of Chaucer on the table before him. [2] Later this spring, during his intensive study of Dryden, he again comes across his favorite poem, *The Flower and the Leaf,* as Gittings has observed. [3] Dryden makes more manifest the latent dream-vision structure of this poem. In his version, subtitled "A Vision," the young woman, while listening to the nightingale's song, is "in a pleasing Dream of Paradice" from which she then wakes; in the pseudo-Chaucerian poem, the woman feels that she is "ravished" into "Paradise," but any implication that she is dreaming is certainly tentative. [4] Later, in a letter of June 1819, Keats slightly misquotes a phrase of *The Legend of Good Women,* writing "ye hear no more of me" rather than Chaucer's "Ye gete no more of me." [5] While some scholars feel that Keats abandoned *The Eve of St. Mark* abruptly in February 1819, [6] he is apparently still considering it in September, although, in a letter to his brother, he prefaces his quotation of the fragment by expressing doubts as to whether he will finish it. [7] Finney suggests that Keats revised the poem at this time and wrote the Chaucerian description of the superstitious beliefs about St. Mark's Eve. [8] In the autumn of 1819, Keats does indicate that he has been reading Chaucer closely enough to object to his "particles" and "gallicisms"; he now prefers Chatterton, he says, as the "purest writer" of English.[9]

We know that Keats had read at least two poems written in the dream-vision form. He had read *The Flower and the Leaf,* whose vision structure is more emphatic in Dryden's version, and he had read Chaucer's *The Legend of Good Women,* which he quotes roughly; the prologue, or first section, of this poem is a dream-vision. Chaucer's other poems in this form are *The Book of the Duchess, The Parliament of Fowls,* and *The House of Fame.* Keats's use of details characteristic of the genre in *The Eve of St. Mark*—and to a certain extent in *The Fall of Hyperion*—indicate that he was probably acquainted with these other dream poems of Chaucer as well.

Dream-vision poems follow a typical narrative pattern.[10] The narrator, the "main character," is the poet himself who is also, usually, a lover or someone who writes and studies about love. In the preliminary, waking, episode, the poet reads a book or observes some natural object—a bird, a flower; he then falls asleep and has an allegorical dream which expands, comments on, or contrasts with the preliminary observation or reading. In the dream the poet typically finds himself in a garden, or in a grove whose trees are then catalogued in detail, and he is given some new perception—often about love—by a guide who is usually allegorical and feminine.

Even the following very brief summaries of Chaucer's vision poems will indicate some of the details of this genre which are found also in *The Eve of St. Mark* and in *The Fall of Hyperion.* In the prologue to *The Legend of Good Women,* the poet tells how he is persuaded to abandon his books in May, so that he can find a daisy, a flower "Fulfilled of al vertu and honour," one that follows the sun, and hates darkness.[11] After watching the daisy until evening, he goes home, falls asleep, and dreams that he is again in the same meadow where he saw the daisy while awake; this time he sees the god of Love and Alceste, a queen, whose white crown "Made hire lyk a daysie for to sene" (224). He waits "stille as any ston" (310) while they approach. The god of Love upbraids him for writing of faithless women; then Alceste, the allegorical development of the daisy's significance ("vertu and honour"), suggests that Chaucer make reparation by writing a poem in praise of virtuous women. In *The Book of the Duchess*, the poet cannot sleep because of an inexplicable "sorwful ymagynacioun" (14), and so he reads a book, a rhymed "romaunce," written by clerks of "olde tyme" (47–54). The book relates the story of a queen who dies of grief after a vision of her drowned husband tells her of his death. The poet then falls asleep and dreams that, in a grove of great trees, he converses with a man who is very sad over the death of his wife, although he apparently will not die in despair as had the queen of the "romaunce." In the preliminary, waking, episode of *The Parliament of Fowls*, the poet again reads an old book, and reads it all day until darkness, as he says, "Berafte me my bok for lak of lyght" (87). The book is Macrobius's *Commentary* on Cicero's *Dream of Scipio*, and it relates the instructions on government and on the "cause of armonye" in the world (63) which Scipio learned in his dream. The poet then falls asleep and passes through a grove whose trees he catalogues (176–82), goes through a garden, and then enters a temple where there is a statue of the god Priapus, and where Venus and "Richesse" disport themselves "in a prive corner" (163–262); at last he arrives at a parliament of symbolic birds presided over by Nature personified as a woman. Here he learns some of the same things Scipio had learned in his dream, except that Christian rather than pagan overtones and implications are now apparent.[12] *The House of Fame* is a somewhat exceptional specimen of the vision form, probably incomplete, although some have argued that it is complete and that its erratic course is a satire on the genre.[13] In a proem the poet expresses doubts about the significance of dreams generally; no one seems to be able to explain them:

> Why that is an avisioun
> And this a revelacioun
> Why this a drem, why that a sweven,
> And noght to every man lyche even;
> Why this a fantome, why these oracles,
> I not; but whoso of these miracles
> The causes knoweth bet then I,
> Devyne he.

[7–14]

We do not see the poet reading a book in this poem, but in a speech—which is quoted by Hunt in *The Feast of the Poets*— a philosophical eagle upbraids Chaucer for having spent so much time reading:

> also domb as any stoon,
> Thou sittest at another book
> Tyl fully daswed ys thy look.
>
> [656–58][14]

The eagle then explains, while carrying the poet through the sky in his claws, that by Jove's grace these scholarly activities which have so "dazed" the poet are now to be given some "recompensacion" by a visit to the House of Fame (661–71).

Aside from the possible verbal reminiscence in *Hyperion* ("quiet as a stone" [1.4]) of a phrase frequent in Chaucer, the poems of Keats which most resemble Chaucer's vision poems are *The Eve of St. Mark* and *The Fall of Hyperion.* In the first poem, Bertha, like the poet-dreamer, is reading an old book, one that has some rhyme, at least in the "pious poesies" (95) written at the bottom of the page; she has been reading all day, and the dusk has "left her dark / Upon the legend of St. Mark" (51–52) just as the evening "berafte" the poet of his book in *The Parliament of Fowls.* The book tells of "swevenis" (99) as Macrobius's Cicero had told of the dream of Scipio, and Bertha like the poet of *The House of Fame* has been reading till she is "dazed" (56). She is called a "poor cheated soul" (69); something not fully explained is troubling her. This does not mean, necessarily, that she is "hoodwinked" like Madeline, in self-isolation from "reality." [15] The reader's malaise is a characteristic which she shares with the narrators of the dream-visions. Like Chaucer in the proem to *The House of Fame*, Keats makes use of an introductory discussion of the nature and value of dreams in *The Fall of Hyperion.* The catalogue of trees (20–21) resembles that in *The Parliament of Fowls.* The feminine guide, Moneta, with her cosmic knowledge as the last of the early gods, is as basic an allegorical figure as the Nature of *The Parliament of Fowls;* when she implies that Keats, the narrator-poet and dreamer, is not all he should be as a poet, she perhaps resembles

Fragmentary Visions: *The Eve of St. Mark*

Alceste, who suggests some improvements to the narrator-poet and dreamer, Chaucer.

And we should not overlook the meter of *The Eve of St. Mark*. Keats had used a four-foot couplet for several shorter pieces, but in all but one of these a seven-syllable line predominates,[16] not the eight-syllable line of *The Eve of St. Mark;* this is his first attempt to use the four-foot couplet for narration. He could have found it so used in two of Chaucer's dream-visions: *The Book of the Duchess* and *The House of Fame*. Keats did borrow the name *Bertha* from Chatterton's *Aella*, as Gittings has observed; but Chaucer's two vision poems are a more likely source of the meter than is Chatterton's "The Unknown Knight," which Gittings has suggested.[17] Chatterton uses a four-foot, eight-line stanza here with a rhyme scheme *a a b b b a c c*,[18] whereas Chaucer employs the four-foot meter in couplets as Keats does.

Perhaps the most significant structural aspect of the vision-poem is the marked break between the two parts, one of which serves as a thematic comment on the other. As D. S. Brewer has observed regarding the preliminary episode—the reading of Scipio's dream—which precedes the allegorical section of *The Parliament of Fowls*, this introductory tale has very little apparent relation to the main action of the poem; and yet it "has as its chief function the suggestion of the 'philosophical' penumbra within which the brighter, more obviously entertaining part of the poem will function."[19] One may object, of course, that this dichotomized structure makes for a poor poem narratively. Perhaps; but enough of the action is similar in the waking and dreaming episodes to provide at least a thematic relationship. The narrative break is after all a "convention" of the form, and at its best this very dichotomy emphasizes the new knowledge gained by the poet in the second episode. The narrative break is used effectively to this end in *The Fall of Hyperion* when the dreamer, after his swoon, finds himself in a temple which bears no local relationship to the preceding arbor. Probably a similar break would have occurred in *The Eve of St. Mark*. To suggest only this much is hardly hazardous in view of the many dream-vision elements in this poem.

It is difficult not to take advantage of the opportunity for conjecture offered by the fragmentary *Eve of St. Mark.* The most frequently quoted projection as to the future action of the poem is Rossetti's speculation that Bertha will find the superstition of St. Mark's Eve realized this very night; she will see the lover with whom she has trifled enter the church and not return —an event which, according to the superstition, signifies his imminent death.[20] Such a development could be expected from the implications of the twelve Chaucerian lines now usually inserted between lines 98 and 99 of the poem. Keats did not indicate where the twelve lines belonged, however, and Woodhouse copied them separately, at the end of the fragment; because of the doubtful status of these lines, it has been suggested by Walter Houghton that the poem would not have developed the superstition at all, but would have related further action to the story of St. Mark's martyrdom, and especially to Bertha's aspirations for a similarly exciting and exotic life—aspirations whose fulfillment she is being "cheated" out of now because of her humdrum life in an uneventful town.[21] Houghton's suggestion does, as he himself emphasizes, explain better than Rossetti's the rather exotic surroundings—the beautiful old book, and the odd "winter screen" with its bizarre portrayals of "monsters," its "Lima mice," and its "legless birds of Paradise" (77–82).

Perhaps the poem is a fragment because there were too many avenues for further narrative exploration. And there may be still another possibility, one quite consistent with the developing dream-vision structure and especially reminiscent of the extravagant satiric adventures of *The House of Fame.* Maybe Keats had *The Eve of St. Mark* in mind while he was working on "The Cap and Bells" in the fall of 1819,[22] since a girl named Bertha figures again in the later fragment. Perhaps Keats had once planned, even in *The Eve of St. Mark,* that Bertha would fall asleep over her book, and then have fantastic visionary adventures. Certainly the narrator, in *The Eve of St. Mark,* does not seem to be taking Bertha entirely seriously; maybe she was to be taken from her book by a counteracting, satiric vision as Chaucer was taken from his studies by the eagle in *The House of Fame.* The narrative voice of "poor cheated soul" is already satiric in its tone of posed, mocking pity. The screen beside Bertha is bizarre, and any ominous portent in her shadow is punctured by the grotesque description of its hovering presence:

> As though some ghostly queen of spades
> Had come to mock behind her back,
> And dance, and ruffle her garments black.
>
> [86–88]

Did Keats, early in 1819, have already in mind Bertha's fantastic adventures with her fairy kindred (in "The Cap and Bells," stanza 44, she is said to be a changeling)? Was he planning for a dream episode (Elfinan, in stanza 58 of "The Cap and Bells," says the book will throw Bertha into a "fainting fit") and for a flight of the imagination as strange and satiric as Chaucer's in *The House of Fame?* On the other hand, the tone of the poem during the description of the town and the initial description of Bertha's reading by the window (24–56) do not suggest any mockery, either oblique or obvious. The tone of the fragment is inconsistent, and the possibilities for further narrative events are perhaps too manifold ever to have structured this piece into a complete poetic whole.

Keats comes much closer in the Hyperion fragments, than in *The Eve of St. Mark,* to incorporating the vision concept into a viable narrative structure. It is true that the formal aspects of *Hyperion* and *The Fall of Hyperion* have proved difficult to evaluate and even to describe; most critics are more certain, for instance, of what *Hyperion* is not than of what it is—it is not an epic. But Keats has so completely redefined the idea of "epic," borrowing and developing some hints from Hazlitt, that even the first fragment, *Hyperion,* is composed largely of monumental figures which exist mainly for the reader's "contemplation" —to use Hazlitt's word—and which are therefore not very well suited to the traditionally epic requirements of action, of objective struggle and encounter. When Keats abandoned the effort to force his statuesque characters and objects into the usual epic conventions, he probably made the right decision; his massive, static characters were in a more appropriate structural context when they became visions in the inquiring and observing consciousness of the dreaming poet-narrator.

Although Keats did not complete his intended poem, the ambitious fragments which resulted are evidence that this unique kind of epic is not necessarily an impossibility. The recasting of the form, in *The Fall of Hyperion,* was helping the poem to become itself. The first fragment, *Hyperion,* begun in the fall of 1818 and probably abandoned by early spring of 1819,[23] is hardly a traditional epic, despite its Miltonic diction. Finney offers philosophical reasons for the change, suggesting that the "humanistic" theme of *Hyperion* and the more "humanitarian" one of the Induction to *The Fall of Hyperion* yielded ultimately an unsuccessful attempt to fuse them into a third version (*The Fall of Hyperion*).[24] But Bridges comes closer to the real difficulty, noting that *Hyperion* lacks the epic's "solid basis of outward event"; and Bate pinpoints the problem by observing that the traditional epic warfare "was hardly the framework for the more individual and inward struggle shaping up."[25] Keats began, perhaps as early as July 1819, to restructure the poem as a "vision" and evidently abandoned the entire Hyperion endeavor in September.[26] The second attempt, resulting in *The Fall of Hyperion,* has not been considered an over-all improvement either by Keats's friends or by later readers; only a few critics have defended his deletions and stylistic changes. Among these, Bush observes that by avoiding the epic battles in his final plan, Keats adopted a method more in harmony "with his symbolic conception of the subject"; Kroeber praises Keats's subordination of the "story" elements, in both Hyperion fragments, to the "requirements of envisioned truth"; Thomas Vogler suggests that Keats, after writing of Apollo's dying into life, recognized that the poem concerned the internal development of a poet, rather than epic action, and so turned to the device of a vision or dream; and Irene Chayes explains the amalgamation of epic and vision, emphasizing the narrator's imaginative development: within a dream-vision poem resembling those of Chaucer, he receives a vision of material for an epic.[27]

The vision structure is an appropriate recasting for a work which has very little action but which does succeed quite well in presenting several memorable, static, visual images such as Hyperion's palace, his chariot, and Moneta's face. The second version enhances the essentially visual quality by drastically minimizing the action. *Hyperion* is not an epic, even though Keats had adopted a few of the external trimmings by starting the poem in the middle of what little action there is, by including an occasional epic simile, and by implying that the major action was to be a battle or perhaps a series of military confrontations between the Titans and the new generation of gods.[28] But the conflict was not developing; Oceanus and Clymene suggest in their speeches (2. 167–243; 2. 247–99) that the older gods must yield to the new, not oppose them, since the "first in beauty should be first in might" (2. 229). There would be no "outward event"—or at least none of martial confrontation; instead, the evolutionary theme of the poem was proceeding by means of prolonged pictures such as Hyperion's palace and his orbed chariot. The overthrow of the old gods, and the rise of the new, is occurring, even in *Hyperion,* by means of the confrontation of recognition, not the confrontation of conflict: Saturn reads his fate in Thea's face, Oceanus reconciles himself to his fate by looking at Neptune, and Clymene by hearing Apollo; Apollo himself is reborn into godhead by looking at Mnemosyne. Very possibly, as de Selincourt has suggested, the major confrontation of Apollo and Hyperion would have been without martial combat; struck by the power of Apollo's beauty, Hyperion would have been unable to resist.[29]

In both fragments Keats was evidently trying to construct an "epic" consisting of huge, static, monumental "images." On his tour during the summer of 1818, he wonders why the mountains of the Isle of Arran "did not beckon Burns to some grand attempt at Epic." Mountains are a rather stationary kind of epic, although they have in common with epic poetry the characteristic of impressive magnitude. In a letter of 21 September 1818, Keats writes of plunging into "abstract images"; later in the same month, he speaks of "those abstractions which are my only life"; again, in July 1819, he is working on "a very abstract Poem," a remark which probably refers to *The Fall of Hyperion.*[30] This word has an unusual connotation when Keats uses it to refer to his poetry. Newell Ford suggests that by an "abstraction," Keats means an image; Caldwell further refines this definition to an "exfoliation of images." [31] Keats's use of *abstract,* and his concept of "abstract images," evidently owe much to Hazlitt's use of *abstract* in connection with *Paradise Lost.* Through his reading of Hazlitt and of *Paradise Lost,* Keats seems to have associated the idea of "abstract images" with objects of massive and awesome proportions, with objects which Hazlitt describes as "epic." The mountains of Arran, since they are large and visually impressive, Keats could easily relate to "some grand attempt at Epic."

Large objects of visual grandeur were apparently on Keats's mind while he was considering *Hyperion.* In October 1818, Keats is obviously not thinking so much about the narrative action of his epic, as about the elemental impressiveness of the mythical figures he wishes to portray. He speaks of "cogitating on the Characters of saturn and Ops," and he affirms: "shapes of epic greatness are stationed around me." [32] He is thinking of "shapes," not actions; the "epic greatness" of these characters is much like the "epic" greatness of the mountains which he commented on during the summer. Keats's use of the word "stationed" in this remark may be related to his more specifically literary explanation of Milton's "stationing":

> Milton in every instance pursues his imagination to the utmost. . . . But in no instance is this sort of perseverance more exemplified than in what may be called his *stationing or statuary.* He is not content with simple description, he must station,—thus here, we not only see how the Birds *'with clang despised the ground,'* but we see them *'under a cloud in prospect.'* So we see Adam *'Fair indeed and tall—under a plantane'*—and so we see Satan *'disfigured—on the Assyrian Mount.'* [33]

This concept of stationing refers to the imagery which surrounds a figure such as Adam or Satan, but it especially refers to the effect which that imagery has on the figure—the effect of stabilizing it in a statuesque posture as though the character being described were a piece of sculpture.

The idea that a poem might consist largely of such statuesque figures Keats probably found in some of Hazlitt's remarks about abstraction and epic poetry. In the first lecture of his series on the English poets, Hazlitt praises the "abstraction" and "intensity" of Dante:

> In all that relates to the descriptive or fanciful part of poetry, he bears no comparision to many who had gone before, or who have come after him; but there is a gloomy abstraction in his conceptions, which lies like a dead weight upon the mind; a benumbing stupor, a breathless awe, from the intensity of the impression. ... He is the severest of all writers, the most hard and impenetrable, the most opposite to the flowery and glittering; who relies most on his own power, and the sense of it in others, and who leaves most room to the imagination of his readers.[34]

Hazlitt sets "abstraction," a "benumbing stupor," and "breathless awe" in opposition to the "flowery and glittering"—an opposition which Keats may particularly have noticed, since he was not eager to repeat the "mawkish" qualities of *Endymion*. The stupor and awe, created by the "intensity of the impression," might easily apply to some of the moments of solemn visual knowledge in *Hyperion* and *The Fall of Hyperion*.

Later in the same series of lectures, Hazlitt specifically associates the abstract with the epic. He notes that whereas Shakespeare presents the immediate agitation and storm of the "dramatic fluctuation of passion," Milton

> on the other hand, takes the imaginative part of passion—that which remains after the event, which the mind reposes on when all is over, which looks upon circumstances from the remotest elevation of thought and fancy, and abstracts them from the world of action to that of contemplation. The objects of dramatic poetry effect us by sympathy . . . ; the objects of epic poetry affect us through the medium of the imagination, by magnitude and distance, by their permanence and universality.[35]

The objects of epic poetry are removed from dramatic action into a realm of contemplation. As examples Hazlitt notes the pyramids of Egypt and the gothic ruins. As a literary example, Hazlitt suggests Satan's address to the sun (*Paradise Lost*, 4. 31 ff); it "has an epic, not a dramatic interest; for though the second person in the dialogue makes no answer and feels no concern, yet the eye of that vast luminary is upon him, like the eye of heaven, and seems conscious of what he says, like an universal presence." [36] Instead of dramatic dialogue, there is only Satan contemplating the sun, and the sun contemplating Satan. After making this distinction between dramatic and epic poetry, Hazlitt asserts: "Dramatic poetry and epic, in their perfection, indeed, approximate to and strengthen one another," and he quotes examples of this successful combination from both Milton and Shakespeare. [37]

Although Hazlitt affirms in 1818 that the greatest poetry is a combination of dramatic action and of the abstract object of contemplation, in his earlier criticism he had been more confident that a long poem of minimal action could yet be interesting; in *The Round Table*, which Keats had been reading a few months before he heard the lectures, Hazlitt says of *Paradise Lost*: "As there is little action in it, the interest is constantly kept up by the beauty and grandeur of the images." For our "contemplation," epic poetry presents "certain objects in themselves grand and beautiful." Here, as in the later lecture, Hazlitt mentions the Egyptian pyramids as examples of what he calls "epic objects"; but in these earlier observations, he suggests that a poem consisting of such objects would be artistically viable: "Now a poem might be constructed almost entirely of such images, of the highest intellectual passion, with little dramatic interest; and it is in this way that Milton has in a great measure constructed his poem. That is not its fault, but its excellence." [38] Apparently, by the time he delivered his lectures on the English poets, Hazlitt had modified his view slightly with regard to the possibility of a poem "constructed almost entirely" of epic objects; whether or not Keats noticed that this remark was missing from the lecture, his representation of objects and characters in both Hyperion fragments gives every indication that he was experimenting along the novel lines suggested by Hazlitt.

An examination of both fragments indicates that in the first version the expansive descriptions, the nondramatic speeches, and the lack of action are working against the form, whereas in the second version, these characteristics fulfill the form. The context of visionary contemplation gives structural support to the magnificently prolonged descriptions of the objects and characters. Perhaps neither "epic" nor "vision" quite adequately describes the poem which Keats was attempting; perhaps, as a new kind of epic, the Hyperion experiment belongs quite solidly in the epic "tradition," if, as Brian Wilkie argues, radical innovations are an essential part of each new epic.[39] Regardless of the label, however, the recasting of the work was a judicious and imaginative restructuring of the material.

Even in *Hyperion,* the lavishly reiterative descriptions indicate that Keats is indeed trying to construct a poem whose epic character is to reside not in grand action, but in the monumental impressiveness of grand objects. The extended quality of some of these descriptions has attracted the attention and praise of many readers. Perkins, for instance, points to the "slow picturing" of Hyperion's palace door (1. 205–12) as an example of a technique "so intrinsic to Keats's poetry"; this technique reflects the poet's desire "to draw out the enjoyment of concrete experience, to slow it down and give it a more massive persistence." [40] Carefully and elaborately wrought images are typical of this poet's style generally, of course, but in *Hyperion,* Keats uses this descriptive technique to an extent which approaches exaggeration. The description of the palace door is only part of the more massive and prolonged description of Hyperion's palace itself; this elaborate, even somewhat repetitious, rendering is perhaps the result of an effort to build up one of those large awesome objects, one that would rival in epic grandeur the pyramids or the gothic ruin which Hazlitt had suggested as examples. The palace is described more than would be strictly necessary to give us a notion of what it looks like; this epic object or "abstract image" is first described in its general character—the way it has been since the ominous portents have "made Hyperion ache":

> His palace bright
> Bastion'd with pyramids of glowing gold,
> And touch'd with shade of bronzed obelisks,
> Glar'd a blood-red through all its thousand courts,
> Arches, and domes, and fiery galleries;
> And all its curtains of Aurorian clouds
> Flush'd angerly: while sometimes eagle's wings,

Unseen before by Gods or wondering men,
Darken'd the place; and neighing steeds were heard,
Not heard before by Gods or wondering men.

[1. 176–85]

Then, after a few lines given to describing the unpleasant incense which Hyperion now breathes from the sacrifices offered to him, the palace is again described, this time as it appears to Hyperion when he enters it each evening:

And so, when harbour'd in the sleepy west,
After the full completion of fair day,—
For rest divine upon exalted couch
And slumber in the arms of melody,
He pac'd away the pleasant hours of ease
With stride colossal, on from hall to hall;
While far within each aisle and deep recess,
His winged minions in close clusters stood,
Amaz'd and full of fear; like anxious men
Who on wide plains gather in panting troops,
When earthquakes jar their battlements and towers.

[1. 190–200]

The halls, aisles, and deep recesses are nearly an architectural restatement of the courts, arches, domes, and galleries mentioned in the first description, except that now we are given a more inward view of the palace as it appears to Hyperion each time he enters it. With "Even now" (1. 201), our attention is directed to a present, specific occasion. As Hyperion enters right now, we are given the longest description, beginning with the opening of the door and ending with the "high towers" of his "own golden region" being jarred as Hyperion stamps his foot and begins his rather panic-stricken speech (1. 205–24).

Hyperion's chariot, the orb of the sun, is similarly intensified, brightened by a glaze of overlaid description. A brief glimpse is given, just before the palace is described, of "Blazing Hyperion on his orbed fire" (1. 166). Nearly thirty lines (1. 269–98), including an effective epic simile, are later lavished on this object, while Hyperion waits restlessly to begin the day. In the first long sentence (1. 269–83), we see the "planet orb of fire" spinning "round in sable curtaining of clouds," and then the simile suggests the "labouring thought" that has been spent on this magnificent and mysterious object for centuries. The second sentence in this extended description (1. 283–89) tells us twice that there are two wings on this orb and that they are now expanding and rising; then we are told that "the dazzling globe maintain'd eclipse," because, as several short sentences (1. 290–95) inform us repeatedly, not even Hyperion himself can disturb or hasten the hours. The third description of the sun relates little that we do not already know:

> Those silver wings expanded sisterly,
> Eager to sail their orb; the porches wide
> Open'd upon the dusk demesnes of night.
>
> [1. 296–98]

We already know that the wings are silver ("fair argent" [1. 284]), that there are two, that they are expanding and rising, and that "the dusk demesnes of night" still surround the sun's orb. Surely this is an example of "intensity," of repeating the blow twice—or even more than twice. The intensity here differs somewhat from that used in *The Eve of St. Agnes,* where a quite varied metaphorical language is used to describe Madeline asleep, for instance; here, except for the one epic simile, what little metaphor there is ("plumes," "sisterly,"), is quite subdued and brief, never radically distracting the reader from the one persistent picture—of the sun, not quickly sketched, but enameled, and reenameled. Whether or not a poem, along the lines suggested by Hazlitt, could be "constructed almost entirely" of such objects as pyramids, gothic ruins, gods' palaces, and suns, Keats is here approximating such a poem.

Hazlitt had suggested that not only certain objects possess this quality of epic grandeur, but some of the speeches of the characters in *Paradise Lost* have "an epic, not a dramatic interest," for there is no real dialogue between the two parties; Satan's "address" to the sun, which Hazlitt referred to as an example, is not really an address: by confronting the sun and recognizing its beauty, Satan discovers—for the first and only time in the poem—the reality of his loss and fault. Whether or not Keats, in devising the speeches of his *Hyperion,* was thinking of Hazlitt or of Milton, these speeches, with a few brief exceptions, do have the epic quality described by Hazlitt; that is, the characters do not talk to one another, but, by confronting each other, make lengthy discoveries about themselves.

Thea's first speech to Saturn, for instance, begins and ends while Saturn is asleep; it is as static and extended as the description of Hyperion's palace or the sun's orb. When Saturn wakes, his much longer speech takes its impetus and content from the "doom" which he sees in Thea's face. In the course of the speech, he asks her several questions, but they are rhetorical and go unanswered; the main purpose of the speech, as of the pictures of the palace and the sun, is simply to give us a picture of the fallen god, Saturn. The speeches of Oceanus and Clymene in book 2 do much the same thing—they give us pictures of the fallen gods, and, through their eyes, pictures of the new Olympian gods. These fallen gods, except for Enceladus, are not proposing action, but simply trying to find out what has happened. They are recognizing themselves as they are, in their fallen state, and in this respect their speeches have the "epic" interest of Satan's speech to the sun; such a speech is a prolonged statement of the character's recognition of himself and has no direct relation to the practicalities of dramatic action. Keats's remark that he is "cogitating" on the characters of Saturn and Ops, indicates the unique emphasis of this poem—an emphasis on the picturing of monumental characters and objects, rather than devising dramatic action to which such characters and objects would be subordinate.

It is only appropriate in such a poem that the critical moments should be ones not of action but of contemplation. Bate has objected that Apollo must "read" his "wondrous lesson" in the silent face of Mnemosyne (3. 111–12). This episode, he feels, "sways dangerously on the brink of the grotesque"; the evolution from ignorance to knowledge is being accomplished "by something close to hypnotism."[41] But the entire poem has been close to hypnotism. The reader has been asked to focus his attention on objects and characters with a steadfast, nearly trancelike, gaze; and the characters themselves have gained whatever knowledge they could, not by conversation, but by *looking* at other characters. Apollo's contemplation of Mnemosyne, and his subsequent acquisition of knowledge, is not an isolated instance, but one which climaxes similar episodes and which is perfectly consistent with everything we have been led to expect from this poem.

The knowledge which Apollo finds in the face of Mnemosyne is the contrasting counterpart of the doom which Saturn finds in Thea's face. Critics have often noted one or the other of these episodes—John M. Murry suggesting a source in *The Excursion* for Apollo's experience, and Ridley a source in *Macbeth*[42]— without noting *both* of the episodes and their positions in the parallel structure which relates the incidents of book 3 to those of book 1. Bloom has observed the "contrary pattern" of book 3 which reverses the movement of the first two books; in the first two, the movement is from godhead to humanization and mortality, while Apollo is moving toward godhead.[43] This pattern is more than a general movement, however; the former gods themselves give us, in book 2, a hint of this structure which is specifically drawn by means of contrasting incident and image.

There is an almost universal lament for the change of tone in book 3 when the young god of the new hierarchy is presented; de Selincourt, however, does defend the often criticized "weak" portrayal of Apollo as necessary in order to show him capable of suffering.[44] Of course the Titans do certainly suffer as well, but the contrasting representation of Apollo is quite consistent with the developing theme, especially as adumbrated by Oceanus and Clymene in their reconciled speeches. Their observations on what they have seen and heard indicate that the new gods have a greater delicacy of beauty—something different from the brute glory of the fallen generation. Oceanus has seen Neptune in his chariot, "foam'd along / By noble winged creatures he hath made," and riding "on the calmed waters" with " a glow of beauty in his eyes" (2. 234–37). Neptune, unlike the older gods, does not have a heavy awesomeness about him. Nor does Apollo's music, as Clymene describes it. She stood on a shore

> Where a sweet clime was breathed from a land
> Of fragrance, quietness, and trees, and flowers.

> Full of calm joy it was, as I of grief;
> Too full of joy and soft delicious warmth.
>
> [2. 263–66]

She is describing the birthplace of Apollo, and her description already foreshadows the more gentle, less ponderous and gloomy, stationing which will be given to Apollo in book 3. Already we have something of the tone of book 3—a "sweet clime," one of "soft delicious warmth," one of quietness, trees, flowers, and a "calm joy" corresponding to the "calmed waters" over which Neptune rode. She sounds the old music of a hollow shell, only to find it surpassed:

> ... from a bowery strand
> Just opposite, an island of the sea,
> There came enchantment with the shifting wind.
>
> [2. 274–76]

From a "bowery strand"—already the description of the "bower" (3. 32) which is Apollo's home in book 3 is being prepared for; it is "Just opposite" the shore on which Clymene is standing, and so of course just opposite in character as well as position to the dominions of the old gods. There is no inconsistent change in the tone of book 3, though there is a change. The change is necessary in order for the stationing given Apollo in book 3 to be consistent with that given him already in book 2. The former gods have observed the contrast of their realm with that of the new gods and have given the reader a preliminary glimpse of the new realm.

The contrast is structurally implied by means of parallel incidents, certainly a favorite device of Keats. In books 1 and 3 a series of images occurs in nearly the same order. Apollo's assumptiom of godhead repeats the sequence of incidents that leads Saturn to recognize his downfall:

Book 1	Book 3
Saturn is "sunken from the healthy breath of morn, / Far from the fiery noon, and eve's one star" (2–4).	Apollo, in the "morning twilight wandered forth," while a "few stars / Were lingering in the heavens" (33–37).

Saturn is beside a stream which is "voiceless" (11).	Apollo is "Beside the osiers of a rivulet" (34), the thrush is singing (37–38), and no place is "Unhaunted by the murmurous noise of waves" (38–40).
A goddess, Thea, visits Saturn (23–33).	A goddess, Mnemosyne, visits Apollo (46).
Thea decides not to wake Saturn to more woe, and so weeps silently while he sleeps (52–71).	Mnemosyne has been the "watcher" of Apollo's "sleep and hours of life" (72); she is sad because he is, and she asks him to tell her the reason for his grief (69–70).
Saturn reads his "doom" in Thea's face (96–97).	Apollo can "read / A wondrous lesson" in Mnemosyne's silent face (111–12).
Saturn asks: "Who had power / To make me desolate?" (102–3).	Apollo asks: "Where is power?" (103).
Saturn realizes that he has changed, that he no longer looks like himself (100–102), and that he has lost his "real self / Somewhere between the throne," and where he sits now (114–15).	Apollo changes because the "Knowledge enormous," including the knowledge of the recent rebellion, "makes a God" of him (113–36).

The contrast is largely in the "surrounding atmosphere of imagery," or the "stationing" given to the two gods; Saturn is in a gloomy, noiseless vale, and Apollo on an island at dawn, filled with the music of the thrush and of murmurous waves. The incidents that occur are quite similar, including the suggestion that both Saturn and Apollo must suffer a sort of death and loss in order for the new reign to begin; Saturn has lost his "real self," and Apollo, we assume, is just gaining his new self as the fragment ends.

Aside from the stationing, then, the two generations of gods are rather alike, and perhaps as this structure developed, Keats realized that whatever his "theme" may have been originally, the poem was working itself into a statement of evolutionary development; similar incidents and images emphasize an evolutionary, genealogical relationship rather than one strictly of combat and conquest. The poem—with its emphasis on static "images"—had been far from a conventional epic in the first place, and this repetitive structure was taking it even further away from the requirements of warlike conflict. It was a poem whose characters, whose magnificent epic objects, whose "events" even, were to be observed, contemplated like monuments. The new gods, at least in the recorded action of the poem, did not fight the old, but were just *there*, different and yet similar as the repetitive design emphasized; the incident and imagery which portrayed the new generation had evolved from the matrix of similar incident and imagery which characterized the old one. This repetitive structure of parallel incident was creating a poem that stood monumentally still; the stillness was further reinforced by the persistently extended descriptions of objects and by the carefully controlled stationing of characters. *Hyperion*, Keats may have realized, was a poem of contemplation, not of action.

The structural restatement of the material, in *The Fall of Hyperion*, gave it a more appropriate context. The second Hyperion fragment is a vision, with literary antecedents in Dante, perhaps in Chaucer's dream poems, and certainly in Keats's own early use of the bardic trance.[45] The new form removes the basically actionless material even further from the ill-suited realm of direct action by placing it at the call of Moneta's memory; and the events become important, not in themselves—as an epic would have required of them—but only in their parallel relationship to the growth of the narrator-poet. If Keats, beginning to identify himself with Apollo, felt that the poem should be recast as a literary vision, in which he as a dreamer would be the narrator, he was imposing no radical structural change. In *The Fall of Hyperion*, the evolving structure of parallel detail is allowed, by the dream form, to repeat and develop itself more fully, and the peculiar sort of "epic" figures and objects are suitably removed even further from the realm of dramatic action to which they never belonged in the first place.

Recast into the vision form in *The Fall of Hyperion,* the impressive figures and objects appear as Moneta manipulates them, and their significance lies mainly in their relationship to the observing consciousness of the narrator-poet. He progresses through three well-defined "stages" as he goes from the garden to the temple and then to the altar, and the very neatness of these structural units solicits the attention of the reader. Perhaps the most prevalent of interpretations is that the arbor, the temple, and the altar correspond to three stages of life—childhood, the awakening to knowledge, and the mature responsibility toward suffering. De Selincourt interprets the poem this way and relates the three stages to the "chambers of life" as Keats defines them in the letter already quoted; Finney's interpretation varies, for he suggests that the arbor is really a "second" stage—not childhood—and that the altar, then, must represent a fourth stage; Chayes argues that the narrator passes a series of "tests," in the process of becoming a poet, first in the garden, then in the temple, and again during his numbness as he observes Saturn and Thea. Perkins and Sperry have observed the parallel imagery occurring in the several stages, and my own discussion owes something to their remarks.[46]

Some critics have suggested that this fragment cannot progress further than it has because the main event, the climactic one of the poet's painful rebirth, has already occurred. Robert Wagner objects to the placement of the "dying into life" sequence so near the beginning of the poem because this forecloses the development of "elementary dramatic suspense." [47] But the poet's rebirth is not the climax; it is only a foreshadowing given in the "Antechamber of this dream" (1. 465). We have in book 3 of *Hyperion* an unfinished sketch of the further rebirth scene which would have aided the poet's understanding of his own painful approach to the altar. And there is in the poem a kind of suspense.

It is a suspense in reverse; that is, the reader is anxiously alerted not because the unfolding of future events is uncertain, but because they *are* certain, being implied in the repetitive structure and therefore painfully anticipated. The major event of the poem is the narrator's own developing self-knowledge, and this knowledge—like Apollo's in book 3 of *Hyperion*—is presented as an anguished struggle from death into life. A symbolic rebirth occurs three times in the fragment, the narrator achieving each time a clearer understanding of himself as a poet and each time moving closer to a visual apprehension of the large legendary figures, the story of whose fall was evidently intended to confirm and explain his own new knowledge. The rebirth episode occurs first in the arbor, then at the steps of the altar, and then as the narrator, conversing with Moneta at the altar, affirms his willingness to "breathe death" with all false poets. The cyclic reiteration of the rebirth episode is apparently occurring for the fourth time as Moneta begins the visionary presentation of the death of the old order of gods.

With each repetition of the rebirth episode, the narrator understands its meaning, and himself, more fully. In the arbor, he hardly ventures to interpret the significance of his surroundings. At the steps of the altar, however, Moneta's announcement that his survival depends on his ascending to the altar gives greater meaning and urgency to the struggle to remain conscious in an environment of deserted magnificence. The third reiteration of the rebirth motif is made verbally by the narrator-poet himself; his knowledge has advanced to the point where he can speak of his own development and can denounce himself along with false poets. With each repetition of the pattern, the narrator's knowledge becomes more explicit, until he is able, along with Moneta, to describe and interpret the visionary figures which she presents.

The arbor is richly, but for the most part directly, described; the narrator uses a few suggestive metaphors, but does not speculate about what the left-over feast means. In retrospect, the architectural metaphors of the arbor's "drooping roof" (1. 25) and "wreathed doorway" (1. 28) seem to be foreshadowing the more solemn edifice of the temple; but the narrator himself, at this stage of his experience, can hardly be expected to foresee in this doorway any of the graver implications of the black gates of the temple which he later finds closed forever against the sunrise. Nevertheless, the narrator's description of the arbor suggests that hs is already dimly aware of some implications of sacrifice and loss; he thinks the blooms of flowers resemble "floral censers swinging light in air" (1. 27), and he notices that the feast consists only of "refuse," of "remnants" from a meal which angels or Eve might have tasted (1. 29–34). Yet the feast is still abundant, containing more than the "fabled horn" could supply "For Proserpine return'd to her own fields" (1. 35–37). The fact that the poet yearns for a feast associated both with Eve's loss and Proserpine's return suggests already that he longs for some kind of rebirth even if it means a kind of death as well.

The drink, which the poet says is "parent" of his theme, probably symbolizes the entry into the poetic trance. It merely symbolizes it, for the entire poem is a dream, of course. The poem is a dream about the meaning of poetic dreams or trances; or, to put it another way, this poem concerns the question of what it means to be a poet and to be capable of such trances and visions. In addition, the grove and the arbor may symbolize the special capacities of the poetic imagination. Here are scented flowers, and

> trees of every clime,
> Palm, myrtle, oak, and sycamore, and beech,
> With Plantane, and spice blossoms. . . .
>
> [1. 19–21]

Addison had observed, in the series of essays on the pleasures of the imagination, that the poet can combine "all the Beauties of the Spring and Autumn" in his descriptions; the soil of an imaginary garden is not restricted "to any particular Sett of Plants, but is proper either for Oaks or Mirtles, and adapts it self to the Products of every Climate." The poet can include a grove of spices, or a new species of flowers "with richer Scents" than any known to nature.[48] Since the grove in *The Fall of Hyperion* contains trees of every climate, it may in itself symbolize the fertile and varied activities of the poetic imagination. When the poet eats, drinks, and swoons, he is experiencing the consequences of his "yearning" (39) for imaginative experience.

The events in the temple are apparently a further elaboration of the meaning of his swoon in the arbor, but the reminiscent imagery now carries more solemn implications. Here the poet begins to understand more fully the meaning of his capacity for visions. The arbor's drooping roof has yielded to an "eternal domed monument" (1. 71), and the remnants of a paradisal feast have become a confused heap of sacrificial vessels and garments: "Robes, golden tongs, censer, and chafing-dish, / Girdles, and chains, and holy jewelries" (1. 79–80). Instead of a feast, the poet approaches a "lofty sacrificial fire" and breathes a powerful incense which

> spread around
> Forgetfulness of everything but bliss,
> And clouded all the altar with soft smoke.
>
> [1. 102–5]

The imagery of the smoke clouding the altar seems to be preparing for another "cloudy swoon" such as the one experienced by the poet after his draught in the arbor; Moneta's words immediately confirm this suspicion: " 'If thou canst not ascend / These steps, die on that marble where thou art' "(1. 107–8). As he had "struggled hard" against the potion in the arbor, the poet here "strove hard to escape / The numbness" (1. 127–28). When he succeeds in gaining the altar's lowest step, his renewed life is described with imagery very similar to that which terminated the arbor scene; there he leaped up "As if with wings," and now he mounts "As once fair Angels on a ladder flew / From the green turf to Heaven" (1. 135–36).

Significantly, this second enactment of the rebirth motif takes place before the huge statue of Saturn. In the arbor, a legendary fall of gods or men had been indicated obliquely by metaphor; in the temple, however, the fallen god himself is concretely represented as "An Image, huge of feature as a cloud" (1. 88). Although the narrator does not yet know Saturn's story, the nearly abandoned temple and the clutter of unused vestments bear witness to the god's fallen status. Saturn is first seen, in this fragment, as a grand piece of statuary, as a mere passive monument, important here mainly because he is observed by the narrator's developing consciousness; Saturn is now a visual image in the poet's trance.

The narrator's perception develops to the point of direct

self-criticism during his earnest conversation with Moneta. Standing at the altar, after his struggle to reach it, the poet asks, "What am I that should so be sav'd from death?" (1. 138). The question verbalizes the rebirth motif for the first time, and the answer, given by the narrator out of his increased understanding, affirms that he is a poet who must yet renounce something in himself; he may have to "breathe death" with the "mock lyrists" in order to find his own "life" as a poet: "Tho' I breathe death with them it will be life / To see them sprawl before me into graves" (1. 209–10). The theme of regeneration, subtly present in the imagery of the arbor episode, and more explicitly indicated by Moneta's urgent words during the narrator's struggle to reach the first step, is now fully present in the narrator's consciousness.

During this third reiteration and elaboration of the rebirth motif, certain aspects of the poet's rather mysterious and only dimly conscious experience in the arbor are clarified. For instance, the draught which the narrator swallowed in the arbor seemed more powerful than the elixirs and poisons of jealous caliphats and monks (1. 47–49). Now Moneta denounces the "dreamers weak" and suggests that the narrator belongs to this "tribe." A dreamer is one who "venoms all his days, / Bearing more woe than all his sins deserve." The people whom Moneta continues to describe are those who, like the monks, poison themselves with an exaggerated sense of woe (1. 162–76). The narrator submits, at least partly, to this identification of himself with these "dreamers"; he is glad to be "favored for unworthiness," and by Moneta's words to be "medicin'd / In sickness not ignoble" (1. 182–84). He objects to a complete identification, however. Since he himself defines the poet as a "Physician" (1. 190) before Moneta defines the poet as one who "pours out a balm upon the world" (1. 201), we can be sure that, even if the narrator feels he is an incomplete poet, he yet recognizes the real one; he is not deceived, and his immediate denunciation of the "mock lyrists, large self-worshipers, / And careless Hectorers" (1. 207–8) indicates that he is willing to sacrifice himself in order to free the world of unworthy poets. His denunciation of such poets, and of himself, to the extent that he too may be a "mock lyrist," is determined, perhaps violent. Edward Bostetter goes too far, however, when he argues that Keats is being "masochistic" here, and that he is as "ruthless" to himself in this poem as Apollonius is to Lycius in *Lamia.* [49] What happens here to the narrator, in his excited dialogue with Moneta, is a rebirth as well as a death; the dialogue represents growth, a development of insight. After all, the narrator calls on Apollo, described in *Hyperion* as the "Father of all verse" (3. 13), and thus the narrator aligns himself with the new generation of gods whose triumph over the old will be the substance of the vision presented to him by Moneta.

It may be that lines 187 through 210 are not the finished statement that Keats wanted; the repetition of the lines describing Moneta's veil, earnest words and pendent censer (1. 194–98 and 1. 216–20), indicates that this section was very much in a state of revision. As a result there has been some contention over whether these lines denouncing the mock lyrists should be considered as part of this fragmentary poem; considered in the light of the reiterative structure which we have been observing, either these lines or something like them[50] should appear about this time. The imagery has again led the poem toward a symbolic scene of the narrator's death and rebirth. While these lines may be less than perfect in themselves, they do nevertheless fulfill exactly the requirement of the poem's structure at this point.

A further repetition of the same series of images is probably beginning for the fourth time as the poet is introduced to the magnificent remnants of the fallen race of gods; Moneta identifies the statue in the temple as Saturn's and reveals her own impressive, wan face. As the poet had yearned for the drink in the arbor, so at the sight of Moneta's face, he "ached to see what things the hollow brain / Behind enwombed" (1. 276–77). He yearns for a greater understanding of himself as a poet, as someone who is capable of visions but who wishes not to be a mere "dreamer"; he wants Moneta to reveal the significance of his regeneration as a poet. Moneta obliges by presenting a vision of the fallen gods whose collapse has made Apollo, and poetry, sovereign in a new world.

In this second version of the poem, the fallen deities are

important chiefly as a visionary aid to the poet's self-knowledge, and their static and pictorial qualities are emphasized even more than in the *Hyperion* fragment. The narrator, who saw the image of Saturn before seeing the god himself, now thinks, as Moneta begins the vision, that he is seeing only another statue:

> Onward I look'd beneath the gloomy boughs,
> And saw, what first I thought an Image huge,
> Like to the Image pedestal'd so high
> In Saturn's Temple.
>
> [1. 297–300]

In this version of the poem, the fallen Saturn is at first actually mistaken for statuary, a circumstance that emphasizes his importance as a visionary monument to the poet's advancing knowledge, rather than as an active character in an epic battle. Saturn's speech here is also changed to make it conform to the new structural context of the narrator's observing and developing mind. In *Hyperion,* Saturn spoke "As with a palsied tongue, and while his beard / Shook horrid with such aspen-malady" (1. 93–94). But in the later fragment, Saturn's words are compared to "the moist scent of flowers, and grass, and leaves," filling "forest dells with a pervading air, / Known to the woodland nostril" (1. 404–6). These reminders of flowers, woods, and fragrance, as Saturn begins to describe his own lost golden world, emphasize the similarity of Saturn's fall to the poet's own symbolic "death" in the arbor. The vision which Moneta is giving to the poet represents a further variation and elaboration of the imagery first used in the description of the garden.

As vision within vision continues, the trance pattern expands; the same "set" of images repeat themselves as the poet's observing consciousness matures. Each reiteration of the series of images probes more thoroughly the narrator's deepening understanding of what it means to drink visionary draughts in imaginary gardens. Within this developing vision, the "epic" figures—which were never intended for an active, narrative, traditional epic—become part of the poet's unfolding self-knowledge.

Moneta has just begun to present the vision which will explain the implications of this self-knowledge and has given the poet a glimpse of Hyperion, when the fragment ends. For this reason, it is difficult to summarize neatly the knowledge which the dreaming poet attains. The structure of the poem implies that this knowledge will be unfolded more fully with each episode in the pattern of repeated images and incidents. Since the pattern is incomplete, the fullest statement of the meaning of the poet's regeneration is never given. And yet, the poet's attitude toward his regeneration has already changed significantly; although we cannot know the "meaning" of the poem, the meaning of the fragment perhaps lies in this changed attitude. As we have seen, when the poet is in the arbor, he does not actively explore it or try to understand its significance. If the drink in the arbor symbolizes his first taste of imaginative experience, then he evidently becomes a poet almost unconsciously, without decision or commitment; he has an appetite and a thirst, and these abruptly transport him to the austere temple. Here he begins to assume responsibility for his continuing growth. He questions, argues, and clarifies his concept of the poet. After each experience of numbness or symbolic death, he is more wide awake, more conscious, and more eager to pursue the struggle. Part of his self-knowledge is this discovery of his own persistence, his commitment to poetry, even if it involves pain, struggle, and the possibility that he may have to "breathe death" (1. 209) in order to become a "poet" instead of a "dreamer."

When the narrator begins to see the visions which Moneta imparts, he has already developed an attitude of willing involvement which he lacked in the arbor. The fragment suggests that with each episode of repeated images, the narrator becomes braver and more willing to understand the implications of being a poet. The fact that Moneta allows him to see the monumental remnants of a divine struggle, which will evidently reflect his own, indicates that the observing narrator has already grown from an unthinking and careless dreamer to a perceptive poet, fully committed to further struggle and knowledge.

Notes

1. For the date of composition, see Garrod, ed., *Poetical Works*, p. 449; for Keats's comment on the Chaucerian lines, see *Letters of John Keats*, 2:204.

2. *Letters of John Keats*, 2:73.

3. Gittings, *John Keats*, p. 317. For internal evidence of Keats's study of Dryden see Bate, *Stylistic Development*, pp. 149–71. Brown remarks that Keats wrote *Lamia* (summer of 1819) with great care "after much study of Dryden" (*Keats Circle*, 2:67).

4. "The Flower and the Leaf: or, The Lady in the Arbour, A Vision," in *The Poems of John Dryden*, James Kinsley, ed., 4 vols. (Oxford: Clarendon Press, 1958), 4:1653. See lines 114–45 for the description of the woman listening to the nightingale's song, and especially line 122: "At length I wak'd." Compare this with the medieval version in which the listener feels entranced by the nightingale's song, but does not fall asleep (*The Floure and the Leafe*, ed. Pearsall, lines 113–19).

5. *Letters of John Keats*, 2:120, and n. 3.

6. Gittings, *John Keats*, p. 289; Ward, *John Keats*, p. 254.

7. *Letters of John Keats*, 2:201; the fragment is quoted on pages 201–4.

8. The lines concerning the superstition seem to have been intended as part of *The Eve of St. Mark*, although Keats did not actually work them into the poem; see Finney, *Evolution of Keats's Poetry*, 2:564–66.

9. *Letters of John Keats*, 2:167, 212. For further references to Chaucer in the poetry and letters of Keats, see F. E. L. Priestley, "Keats and Chaucer," p. 439; and Alexander H. Sackton, "A Note on Keats and Chaucer," *Modern Language Quarterly* 13 (March 1952): 37–40. Sackton discusses the opening lines of *Lamia*, which are reminiscent of the beginning of Chaucer's *Wife of Bath's Tale*.

10. For discussions of the formal characteristics of this genre, see Wilber Sypherd, *Studies In Chaucer's Hous of Fame*, Chaucer Society, 2d ser., no. 39 (London, 1907 [for 1904]); and D. S. Brewer, ed., *The Parlement of Foulys* (London and Edinburgh: Thomas Nelson and Sons, 1960), pp. 8–10.

11. The Prologue to *The Legend of Good Women*, in *The Works of Geoffrey Chaucer*, ed. F. N. Robinson, 2d ed. (Boston: Houghton Mifflin Co., 1961), p. 483, *F* text, lines 54, 63. The Prologue exists in two versions, designated *F* and *G* by Robinson; the *G* text exists in only one manuscript and was not printed until 1871 (see ibid., pp. 839–40). All quotations of Chaucer's vision poems will be from this edition and will be cited by line number in the text; quotations of the Prologue to *The Legend of Good Women* will be from the *F* version.

12. I am following Brewer's interpretation here; see his edition of *The Parlement of Foulys*, pp. 18, 21.

13. Wilber Sypherd, "The Completeness of Chaucer's *Hous of Fame*," *Modern Language Notes* 30 (March 1915): 65–68.

14. Hunt, *Feast of the Poets*, p. 121.

15. Stillinger, *The Hoodwinking of Madeline*, pp. 94–98. Far from being "hoodwinked," Bertha may be enjoying, imaginatively, a more real world than the narrow one of church and superstition; see David Luke, "*The Eve of St. Mark*: Keats's 'ghostly Queen of Spades' and the Textual Superstition," *Studies in Romanticism* 9 (1970): 161–75.

16. In all of the following except "Fill for me a brimming bowl," a seven-syllable line predominates, not the eight-syllable one of *The Eve of St. Mark:*

Lines on the Mermaid Tavern	Bards of Passion and of Mirth
Fancy	Robin Hood
Fill for me a brimming bowl	Song of Four Fairies
Hadst thou lived in days of old	Not Aladdin magian

17. Robert Gittings, *The Mask of Keats: A Study of Problems* (London: William Heinemann, 1965), p. 95.

18. See *The Poetical Works of Thomas Chatterton*, ed. Walter W. Skeat, 2 vols. (London: George Bell and Sons, 1891), 2:247 ff. Chatterton does use rhymed tetrameter couplets, which he describes as "Hudibrastics," for several satiric poems, most of them quite brief; see ibid., 1:42, and poems beginning on pp. 4, 6, 7, 33, 192.

19. Brewer, ed., *The Parlement of Foulys*, p. 17.

20. For Rossetti's statement see Hampstead Keats, 4:177–78.

21. Walter E. Houghton, "The Meaning of Keats's *Eve of St. Mark*," *ELH* 13 (March 1946): 64–78.

22. For discussion of the probable date of composition, see de Selincourt, ed., *Poems of John Keats*, p. 559.

23. The majority of scholars agree that *Hyperion* was begun in the fall of 1818. See Garrod, *Keats*, pp. 48–49; Bate, *John Keats*, p. 392; de Selincourt, ed., *Poems of John Keats*, pp. 484–85. Keats probably abandoned this version by February, for he writes to George: "I have not gone on with Hyperion" (*Letters of John Keats*, 2:62), although Ward suggests that he did write of Apollo's transformation in March (*John Keats*, pp. 263–65).

24. Finney, *Evolution of Keats's Poetry*, 2:454–69.

25. Bridges, *Collected Essays*, 4:107; Bate, *John Keats*, p. 407.

26. Keats's reference to a very "abstract" poem in July 1819 (*Letters of John Keats*, 2:132) is interpreted by some critics to mean that he has begun work on *The Fall of Hyperion*. See Bate, *John Keats*, p. 563; and Ridley, *Keats' Craftsmanship*, pp. 58–59. Brown records that Keats was busy in the fall of 1819 remodeling the Hyperion poem into a "Vision"; see *Keats Circle*, 2:72. Keats writes to Reynolds on 21 September 1819, that he has "given up Hyperion" (*Letters of John Keats*, 2:167), a statement which most scholars interpret as referring

to *The Fall of Hyperion*, that is, to the abandoning of the entire Hyperion project.

27. Bush, *Mythology and the Romantic Tradition*, p. 119; Kroeber, *Romantic Narrative Art*, p. 111; Thomas A. Vogler, *Preludes to Vision* (Berkeley and Los Angeles: University of California Press, 1971), pp. 123–24; Irene Chayes, "Dreamer, Poet, and Poem in *The Fall of Hyperion*," *Philological Quarterly* 46 (1967):499–515.

28. Gittings agrees with Woodhouse's annotations that Keats planned to represent the dethronement of the important older gods one by one (*John Keats*, pp. 331–32, and n. 1); de Selincourt thinks that Keats, at the time of composition, already had modified the scheme as Woodhouse understood it and that the poem would have included no actual military confrontations (*Poems of John Keats*, pp. 486–89).

29. De Selincourt, ed., *Poems of John Keats*, p. 488.

30. *Letters of John Keats*, 1:331, 369, 370, and 2:132; see note 26 above for interpretation of the reference to an "abstract poem."

31. Ford, *Prefigurative Imagination of John Keats*, p. 23 n. 4; Caldwell, *Keats' Fancy*, p. 150.

32. *Letters of John Keats*, 1:387, 403.

33. Hampstead Keats, 5:303–4.

34. *Hazlitt Works*, 5:17.

35. Ibid., p. 52. Hazlitt uses the word *abstract* and its relatives in several contexts; his "revolutionary" redefinition of the process of "abstraction" as one which proceeds from generalization to individuation has been examined by Roy Park in "The Painter as Critic: Hazlitt's Theory of Abstraction," *PMLA* 85 (October 1970):1072–81.

36. *Hazlitt Works*, 5:52.

37. Ibid., pp. 52–53.

38. Ibid., 4:106, 110. Helen Darbishire suggests that Keats may have modeled Saturn, Thea, Hyperion, and perhaps Moneta's face, on Egyptian sculpture; see "Keats and Egypt," *Review of English Studies* 3 (January 1927):1–11. Ian Jack, quoting Keats's references to a "Sphinx" *(Letters of John Keats*, 2:68), feels that he may have seen the head of Rameses II, then at the British Museum; see Jack's *Keats and the Mirror of Art* (Oxford: Clarendon Press, 1967), pp. 167–69.

39. Brian Wilkie, *Romantic Poets and Epic Tradition* (Madison and Milwaukee: University of Wisconsin Press, 1965), pp. 3–14.

40. Perkins, *Quest for Permanence*, p. 212.

41. Bate, *John Keats*, pp. 404–5.

42. Murry, *Mystery of Keats*, pp. 223–24 (*Excursion*, 1. 203–5 and 2. 40–41); Ridley, *Keats' Craftsmanship*, p. 92 (*Macbeth*, 1. 5. 63).

43. Bloom, *Visionary Company*, pp. 394–95.

44. De Selincourt, ed., *Poems of John Keats*, pp. 512–13.

45. See for the influence of Dante: Gittings, *Mask of Keats*, pp. 38–39; John Livingston Lowes, " 'Hyperion' and the 'Purgatorio'," *Times Literary Supplement*, 11 January 1936, p. 35. Bridges in *Collected Essays*, 4:113, asserts that *The Fall of Hyperion* shows some

echoes of Dante's Italian; so also says John Saly, "Keats's Answer to Dante: *The Fall of Hyperion*," *Keats-Shelley Journal* 14 (Winter 1965):65–78.

46. De Selincourt, ed., *Poems of John Keats*, pp. 516–17; Finney, *Evolution of Keats's Poetry*, 2:462–66; Chayes, "Dreamer, Poet, and Poem in *The Fall of Hyperion*," pp. 508–13; Perkins, *Quest for Permanence*, p. 281; Sperry, *Keats the Poet*, pp. 321–23. See the letter to Reynolds, 3 May 1818 (*Letters of John Keats*, 1:280–81), which was quoted above, chap. 2, pp. 19–20.

47. Robert D. Wagner, "Keats: 'Ode to Psyche' and the Second 'Hyperion,' " *Keats-Shelley Journal* 13 (Winter 1964):36. See also Bate who observes that Keats typically begins a poem by putting "the best of what he could do at the start" (*John Keats*, p. 602).

48. Addison, *The Spectator*, 3:569.

49. Edward Bostetter, *The Romantic Ventriloquists*, pp. 168, 166.

50. Ridley agrees with de Selincourt that either these lines or something like them are needed here to complete the argument (Ridley, *Keats' Craftsmanship*, p. 273; de Selincourt, ed., *Poems of John Keats*, pp. 518–19). Others regard the lines as unnecessary, or as contradictory to the rest of the poem. See Murry, *Mystery of Keats*, pp. 192–95; Finney, *Evolution of Keats's Poetry*, 2:459; Bate, *John Keats*, pp. 599–600; Wagner, "Keats: 'Ode to Psyche' and the Second 'Hyperion,' " pp. 40–41.

VII

A Test of Invention

To the challenge of narrative verse Keats brought the same sensitive imagination which readers have always recognized in his shorter poems. His ambition to write a long work yielded several tests of his invention, and in each test, each attempt, he explored new ground. Sometimes his search for structure resulted in artificial or rather self-conscious modes of incorporating a world into his poem; in *Isabella* the rhetorical denunciation of the murderous brothers interrupts the form instead of contributing to it. In other poems, however, the structuring elements themselves imply the context of value, the world in which the characters live and by which they can be understood. In *The Eve of St. Agnes* and *Lamia,* and to some extent in *Hyperion* and *The Fall of Hyperion,* Keats provides, as Hazlitt had urged, "all the possible associations"; he synthesizes the "Magnitude of Contrast"—a quality which he admired in *Paradise Lost*—into a complete whole.

Even in his early explorations of structure in the 1817 volume, Keats sometimes integrates value and form. In the first "Endymion" poem—"I Stood Tip-Toe"—Keats extends the implications of certain objects in the landscape by means of a repetitive structure in which external images become images in the poet's mind. In this poem, and in the vision sections of the epistle to George Keats, the structure of the bardic trance shapes the form and simultaneously shapes the musing narrator's desire to become a poet. Meaning and form join in a single imaginative whole. This structure of repeated images, although minimal and lacking in subtlety, gave direction and meaning to poems which might otherwise have succumbed utterly to an overindulgence in the luxuriant "variety" celebrated by Hunt in his "feast" of poets. The rudimentary pattern of repeated images provided a kind of staple among Hunt's delicacies. Keats seems to have found the basic form a useful and flexible one, for he continued to experiment with it in his later poems.

The very real limits of this structure become apparent when it is extended over the four thousand lines of *Endymion.* The scaffolding is almost too flimsy to support the voluminous weight of embellishment. Nevertheless, this pattern does give the poem its shape and sense. The hero's visions are gradually fulfilled as he proceeds in an adventure which mirrors his visions. The complexities and vagaries of the fairy way of writing decorate the form almost to the extent of obscuring it, but the large comprehensive design of the poem does give this test of invention a boundary and a meaning. *Endymion* is more than mere imaginative gymnastics; Keats's goal was not just an arbitrary four thousand lines, but a poem. The result is a carefully maintained large structure and a less successfully executed interior; the heavy decor of the poem puts severe stress on the very grand design. The design is, however, an appropriate one for the hero's quest. The structure of the poem adumbrates the happy fulfillment of his search. Quest and structure reinforce each other as Endymion finds that the earthly beauty of the Indian Maid can also respond to his question about his divine destiny; the transformation of the Indian Maid into Cynthia is the culmination of Endymion's long search for the union of vision and reality, a union which the mirror structure of the poem implies.

With *Isabella* Keats begins to sculpture a narrative by means of imagery; he shapes events into a climax by controlling the poem's visual and emotional intensity. Both his achievements and his failures in *Isabella* are the result of quite deliberate efforts to forgo the expansive fairy way; instead, he tests his invention on the "natural" subject matter of the story of Isabella. Keats probably observed Hazlitt's praise of Boccaccio's tale and particularly this critic's assertion that a natural subject provides a great stimulus to imagination. The influence of Hazlitt during this period, along with Keats's reading of Shakespeare and Milton, encouraged a renewed experimentation with narrative structures. Evidently heeding Hazlitt's reservations about an "infinite quantity of dramatic invention," Keats turned his attention to the structural implications of "gusto" and "intensity." The most important axiom which he developed at this time, and which probably owed something to Hazlitt, is the structural concept of making the imagery rise and set. Although *Isabella*, as a narrative experiment, is not entirely successful, it does demonstrate Keats's first attempt to orchestrate character and suspense by means of modulating the imagery. It is his first, tentative adventure into the lyric narrative.

The subtly controlled imagery of *The Eve of St. Agnes* demonstrates Keats's mastery of the lyric narrative and his ability to embody a context of value in the structural framework of the poem. *The Eve of St. Agnes*, famous for its moments of sensuous description, deserves attention also for the rising imagery which builds toward the climactic feast and love-making. The meaningful narrative whole which Keats builds in this poem depends on the imagery's linear development and on the context of rising suspense which gives to the meeting of Madeline and Porphyro its special power. To praise two or three stanzas as isolated gems of Keats's glittering style is to do him an injustice; such a response implies that Keats, when he writes narrative verse, is good only by accident, only as a result of his lyric ability having managed to interrupt the narrative mode. By the time he wrote *The Eve of St. Agnes*, however, Keats understood his medium. He does not abandon suspense or character delineation; he simply creates these things in a new way. He implies suspense, not so much by action, as by the "surrounding atmosphere" of imagery. By the same means he also gives subtle characterization to the major figures of the poem and adroitly shapes the reader's emotional response to them.

Keats's response to the ballad form, in *La Belle Dame sans Merci*, demonstrates the flexibility of lyric narration; in this poem, Keats noticeably restrains his imagery, never allowing the kind of heavy piling up of metaphor which he had used in *The Eve of St. Agnes*. He lets the traditionally bare style of the ballad work for him. He increases the mysteriousness of the fairy woman by giving her an especially restricted, low-key description. By the same means and by allowing the knight to be more vividly portrayed, Keats structurally implies the central significance of the poem's action: the knight's own gestures and his own imagination are largely responsible for his enthrallment. The knight proceeds to interpret and, in a sense, to characterize a figure whom the poet himself only sketches in, refusing to clarify her mystery.

In *Lamia,* Keats adapts the elements of lyric narration to another strange and ambiguous female character. Employing again a repetitive structure similar to that used in *Endymion,* Keats subtly allows the double form to mirror the duplicity of Lamia. The frequently praised brilliant passages in this poem are brilliant in relation to Lamia; Lycius is not given such a vivid aura of imagery, and Apollonius is glimpsed in quick cool descriptions that emphasize his stern rational eye. The imagery rises when Lamia is present. Her magical presence is the impetus for the most vivid passages; she in a sense creates them, and certainly they represent her capacity to construct an illusory world. As she fades, under the gaze of Apollonius, the imagery sets. Keats is very much in control of the form here, skillfully meshing lyric and narrative modes into one poetic medium.

Keats returns to the concept of vision, briefly, in *The Eve of St. Mark,* and more thoroughly in the two Hyperion fragments. Along with the structure of the bardic trance, he evidently experiments with some aspects of the Chaucerian dream-vision, particularly in *The Eve of St. Mark* and in *The Fall of Hyperion.* The Chaucerian dream-vision and the bardic trance have in common the structure of repetition with variation; Keats uses this structure in *The Fall of Hyperion* to indicate the narrator's continually developing knowledge of the one basic event of the poem, his regeneration as a poet. Although Keats initially attempted to embody in traditional epic conventions his magnificent, highly visual, and static characters, he found such conventions to be inappropriate. The monumental stillness of this peculiar "epic" is intensified by the importance which Keats gives to the huge, impressive "abstract images," the "shapes of epic greatness." When he revised *Hyperion* as a vision, he could work with a more suitable form. Developing some tentative remarks of Hazlitt concerning an epic of objects rather than events, Keats exploits an innovative structure, one certainly appropriate to a long poem dealing with the narrator-poet's visionary experience of his own psychological rebirth. Since perception is more important than action in *The Fall of Hyperion,* the implied linear development is only a beautiful finesse which continually redirects the reader's attention to the narrator's more and more conscious commitment to becoming a poet rather than a dreamer.

Like the narrator in *The Fall of Hyperion,* Keats himself shows a determined dedication to explore and grow as a poet, and especially as a narrative poet; he after all wished to define himself as a "great" poet, as one who writes "long" works. His sensitive flexibility with regard to form shows the same receptivity, the same open, exploratory imagination which readers have often recognized in his letters and in his short poems. In his longer works he exploits, rejects, or accepts large designs as he continues his search for the most effective way of realizing his one great aim. When he succeeds in this ambition, he really tests more than his invention; he tests his humanity. He tests the scope and intelligence of his response to values by meshing them with the narrative structure itself, weighting and shaping character and action. Writing poetry in an era when both history and literature seemed new, Keats accepted the special risks and challenges of attempting long works in such an age. At its best, his invention integrates value and form, meaning and structure, the poem and its implied world.

List of Works Cited

Texts

Chatterton, Thomas. *The Poetical Works of Thomas Chatterton.* Edited by Walter W. Skeat. 2 vols. London: George Bell and Sons, 1891.

Chaucer, Geoffrey. *The Works of Geoffrey Chaucer.* Edited by F. N. Robinson. 2d ed. Boston: Houghton Mifflin Co., 1961.

Coleridge, Samuel Taylor. *The Annotated Ancient Mariner.* Edited by Martin Gardner. New York: Clarkson N. Potter, 1965.

Drayton, Michael. *Poems of Michael Drayton.* Edited by John Buxton. 2 vols. London: Routledge and Kegan Paul, 1953.

Dryden, John. *The Poems of John Dryden.* Edited by James Kinsley. 4 vols. Oxford: Clarendon Press, 1958.

Hazlitt, William. *The Complete Works of William Hazlitt.* Edited by P. P. Howe. 21 vols. London: J. M. Dent and Sons, 1930–34.

Hunt, Leigh. *The Feast of the Poets, with Notes and Other Pieces in Verse.* London, 1814.

————. *The Poetical Works of Leigh Hunt.* Edited by H. S. Milford. London: Oxford University Press, 1923.

————, ed. *Imagination and Fancy; or Selections from the English Poets.* London: Smith, Elder, and Co., 1844.

Keats, John. *The Letters of John Keats.* Edited by Hyder Edward Rollins. 2 vols. Cambridge, Mass.: Harvard University Press, 1958.

————. *The Poems of John Keats.* Edited by Ernest de Selincourt. London: Methuen and Co., 1920.

————. *The Poetical Works of John Keats.* Edited by H. W. Garrod. 2d ed. London: Oxford University Press, 1958.

————. *The Poetical Works and Other Writings of John Keats.* Edited by Maurice Buxton Forman. The Hampstead edition. 8 vols. New York: Charles Scribner's Sons, 1938–39.

Rogers, Samuel. *Poems.* London: Printed for T. Cadell, 1827.

Virgil. *The Aeneid.* Translated by C. Day Lewis. New York: Doubleday and Co., Anchor Books, 1953.

Works Cited

Wordsworth, William. *The Poetical Works of William Wordsworth.* Edited by Ernest de Selincourt and Helen Darbishire. 5 vols. Oxford: Clarendon Press, 1940–49.

———. *The Prelude, or Growth of a Poet's Mind.* Edited by Ernest de Selincourt. 2d ed. Revised by Helen Darbishire. Oxford: Clarendon Press, 1959.

———, and Coleridge, S. T. *Lyrical Ballads: The Text of the 1789 Edition with the Additional 1800 Poems and the Prefaces.* Edited by R. L. Brett and A. R. Jones. London: Methuen and Co., 1963.

Criticism

Abrams, M. H. *The Mirror and the Lamp: Romantic Theory and the Critical Tradition.* New York: Oxford University Press, 1953.

Addison, Joseph. *The Spectator.* Edited by Donald F. Bond. 5 vols. Oxford: Clarendon Press, 1965.

Alison, Archibald. *Essays on the Nature and Principles of Taste.* Edinburg: Bell and Bradfute; London: J. J. G. and G. Robinson, 1790.

Allen, Glen O. "The Fall of Endymion: A Study of Keats's Intellectual Growth." *Keats-Shelley Journal* 6 (1957):37–57.

Amarasinghe, Upali. *Dryden and Pope in the Early Nineteenth Century.* Cambridge: At the University Press, 1962.

Bate, Walter Jackson. *John Keats.* Cambridge, Mass.: Harvard University Press, Belknap Press, 1963.

———. *The Stylistic Development of John Keats.* New York: Modern Language Association of America, 1945.

Blackstone, Bernard. *The Consecrated Urn: An Interpretation of Keats in Terms of Growth and Form.* London: Longmans, Green, and Co., 1959.

Bloom, Harold. "The Internalization of Quest Romance." *Yale Review* 58 (1969):526–36.

———. *The Visionary Company: A Reading of English Romantic Poetry.* 2d ed., rev. and enl. Ithaca and London: Cornell University Press, 1971.

Bornstein, George. "Keats's Concept of the Ethereal." *Keats-Shelley Journal* 18 (1969):97–106.

Bostetter, Edward. *The Romantic Ventriloquists: Wordsworth, Coleridge, Keats, Shelley, Byron.* Seattle: University of Washington Press, 1963.

Bradley, A. C. *Oxford Lectures on Poetry.* London: Macmillan and Co., 1926.

Brewer, D. S., ed. *The Parlement of Foulys, by Geoffrey Chaucer.* London and Edinburgh: Thomas Nelson and Sons, 1960.

Bridges, Robert. *Collected Essays and Papers.* 10 vols. London: Oxford University Press, 1929.

Works Cited

Bush, Douglas. *Mythology and the Romantic Tradition in English Poetry.* New York: Pageant Book Co., 1957.

Caldwell, James Ralston. *John Keats' Fancy: The Effect on Keats of the Psychology of His Day.* Ithaca, N.Y.: Cornell University Press, 1945.

Chayes, Irene H. "Dreamer, Poet, and Poem in *The Fall of Hyperion.*" *Philological Quarterly* 46 (1967):499–515.

Clarke, Charles and Mary Cowden Clarke. *Recollections of Writers.* New York: Charles Scribner's Sons, 1878.

Cohen, Jane R. "Keats's Humor in 'La Belle Dame sans Merci.'" *Keats-Shelley Journal* 17 (1968):10–13.

Colvin, Sidney. *John Keats.* New York: Charles Scribner's Sons, 1917.

Darbishire, Helen. "Keats and Egypt." *Review of English Studies* 3 (January 1927):1–11.

D'Avanzo, Mario L. *Keats's Metaphors for the Poetic Imagination.* Durham, N.C.: Duke University Press, 1967.

Dunbar, Georgia S. "The Significance of Humor in 'Lamia.'" *Keats-Shelley Journal* 8 (1959):17–26.

Evert, Walter H. *Aesthetic and Myth in the Poetry of Keats.* Princeton, N.J.: Princeton University Press, 1965.

Examiner. Nos. 399 (20 August 1815), 428 (26 May 1816), 435 (28 April 1816), 444 (30 June 1816), 452 (25 August 1816).

Ferguson, Oliver W. "Warton and Keats: Two Views of Melancholy." *Keats-Shelley Journal* 18 (1969):12–15.

Finney, Claude Lee. *The Evolution of Keats's Poetry.* 2 vols. Cambridge, Mass.: Harvard University Press, 1936.

Fogle, Richard Harter. *The Imagery of Keats and Shelley: A Comparative Study.* Chapel Hill, N.C.: University of North Carolina Press, 1949.

Ford, Newell F. *"Endymion*—A Neo-Platonic Allegory?" *ELH* 14 (March 1947):64–76.

———. "The Meaning of 'Fellowship with Essence' in *Endymion.*" *PMLA* 62 (1947):1062–76.

———. *The Prefigurative Imagination of John Keats.* Hamden, Conn.: Archon Books, 1966.

Friedman, Albert B. *The Ballad Revival.* Chicago: University of Chicago Press, 1961.

Garrod, H. W. *Keats.* 2d ed. Oxford: Clarendon Press, 1939.

Gerould, Gordon Hall. *The Ballad of Tradition.* Oxford: Clarendon Press, 1932.

Gittings, Robert. *John Keats.* Boston: Little, Brown and Co., 1968.

———. *The Mask of Keats: A Study of Problems.* London: William Heinemann, 1965.

Goldberg, Milton A. *The Poetics of Romanticism: Toward a Reading of John Keats.* Yellow Springs, Ohio: Antioch Press, 1969.

Green, David Bonnell. "Keats and 'The Spectator.'" *Notes and Queries* 2 (March 1955):124.

Works Cited

Harrison, Robert. "Symbolism of the Cyclical Myth in *Endymion*." *Texas Studies in Literature and Language* 1 (Winter 1960):540–51.

Hartley, David. *Observations on Man, His Frame, His Duty, and His Expectations.* 2 vols. 1749. Facsimile. New York: Garland Publishing, 1971.

Havens, Raymond D. *The Influence of Milton on English Poetry.* Cambridge, Mass.: Harvard University Press, 1922.

Haworth, Helen E. "Keats and the Metaphor of Vision." *Journal of English and Germanic Philology* 67 (July 1968):371–94.

Houghton, Walter E. "The Meaning of Keats's *Eve of St. Mark*." *ELH* 13 (March 1946):64–78.

Jack, Ian. *Keats and the Mirror of Art.* Oxford: Clarendon Press, 1967.

James, D. G. *The Romantic Comedy.* London and New York: Oxford University Press, 1948.

Jones, John. *John Keats's Dream of Truth.* London: Chatto and Windus, 1969.

Kroeber, Karl. *Romantic Narrative Art.* Madison: University of Wisconsin Press, 1960.

Lovejoy, Arthur O. *Essays in the History of Ideas.* Baltimore: Johns Hopkins Press, 1948.

Lowell, Amy. *John Keats.* 2 vols. Boston: Houghton Mifflin Co., 1925.

Lowes, John Livingston. "'Hyperion' and the 'Purgatorio.'" *Times Literary Supplement,* 11 January 1936, p. 35.

Luke, David. "*The Eve of St. Mark:* Keats's 'ghostly Queen of Spades' and the Textual Superstition." *Studies in Romanticism* 9 (1970): 161–75.

Margolis, John. "Keats's 'Men of Genius' and 'Men of Power.'" *Texas Studies in Literature and Language* 11 (1970):1333–47.

Miller, Bruce E. "On The Meaning of Keats's *Endymion*." *Keats-Shelley Journal* 14 (1965):33–54.

Monk, Samuel S. *The Sublime: A Study of Critical Theories in Eighteenth-Century England.* Ann Arbor: University of Michigan Press, 1960.

Muir, Kenneth, ed. *John Keats: A Reassessment.* Liverpool: Liverpool University Press, 1959.

Murry, John Middleton. *Keats.* New York: Noonday Press, 1955.

———. *The Mystery of Keats.* London: Peter Neville, 1949.

O'Hara, J. D. "Hazlitt and Romantic Criticism of the Fine Arts," *Journal of Aesthetics and Art Criticism* 27 (1968):73–85.

Park, Roy. "The Painter As Critic: Hazlitt's Theory of Abstraction." *PMLA* 85 (1970): 1072–81.

Patterson, Charles I., Jr. *The Daemonic in the Poetry of John Keats.* Urbana: University of Illinois Press, 1970.

Pearsall, D. A., ed. *The Floure and the Leafe, and the Assembly of Ladies.* London and Edinburgh: Thomas Nelson and Sons, 1962.

Perkins, David. *The Quest for Permanence.* Cambridge, Mass.: Harvard University Press, 1959.

Works Cited

Pettet, E. C. *On the Poetry of Keats.* London: Cambridge University Press, 1957.

Piper, H. W. *The Active Universe: Pantheism and the Concept of Imagination in the English Romantic Poets.* London: University of London, Athlone Press, 1962.

Priestley, F. E. L. "Keats and Chaucer." *Modern Language Quarterly* 5 (1944):439–47

Randall, John Herman, Jr. *The Making of the Modern Mind: A Survey of the Intellectual Background of the Present Age.* Boston: Houghton Mifflin Co., 1968.

Rauber, D. R. "The Fragment as Romantic Form." *Modern Language Quarterly* 30 (1969):212–21.

Reiman, Donald H. "Keats and the Humanistic Paradox: Mythological History in *Lamia.*" *Studies in English Literature, 1500–1900* 11 (1971):659–69.

Ridley, M. R. *Keats' Craftsmanship: A Study in Poetic Development.* Oxford: Clarendon Press, 1933.

Rollins, Hyder Edward, ed. *The Keats Circle.* 2 vols. Cambridge, Mass.: Harvard University Press, 1948.

Sackton, Alexander H. "A Note on Keats and Chaucer." *Modern Language Quarterly* 13 (March 1952):37–40.

Saly, John. "Keats's Answer to Dante: *The Fall of Hyperion.*" *Keats-Shelley Journal* 14 (Winter 1965):65–78.

Severs, J. Burke. "Keats's 'Mansion of Many Apartments,' *Sleep and Poetry,* and *Tintern Abbey.*" *Modern Language Quarterly* 20 (1959):128–32.

Sheats, Paul D. "Stylistic Discipline in *The Fall of Hyperion.*" *Keats-Shelley Journal* 17 (1968):75–88.

Sikes, Herschel. "The Poetic Theory and Practice of Keats: The Record of a Debt to Hazlitt." *Philological Quarterly* 38 (October 1959): 401–12.

Slote, Bernice. "The Climate of Keats's 'La Belle Dame sans Merci.'" *Modern Language Quarterly* 21 (1960), 195–207.

_____. *Keats and the Dramatic Principle.* Lincoln: University of Nebraska Press, 1958.

_____. "La Belle Dame as Naiad." *Journal of English and Germanic Philology* 60 (January 1961):22–30.

Sperry, Stuart M. *Keats the Poet.* Princeton: Princeton University Press, 1973.

Spurgeon, Caroline. *Keats's Shakespeare.* London: Oxford University Press, 1928.

Stevenson, Lionel. "The Mystique of Romantic Narrative Poetry." In *Romantic and Victorian: Studies in Memory of William H. Marshall,* edited by Paul Elledge and Richard L. Hoffman. Cranbury, N.J.: Fairleigh Dickinson University Press, 1971.

Works Cited

Stevenson, Warren. "*Lamia:* A Stab at the Gordian Knot." *Studies in Romanticism* 11 (1972):241–52.

Stillinger, Jack. *The Hoodwinking of Madeline, and Other Essays on Keats's Poems.* Urbana and Chicago: University of Illinois Press, 1971.

Sypherd, Wilber. "The Completeness of Chaucer's *Hous of Fame.*" *Modern Language Notes* 30 (1915):65–68.

_____. *Studies In Chaucer's Hous of Fame.* Chaucer Society, 2d ser., no. 39. London, 1907 (for 1904).

Thorpe, Clarence D. "Keats and Hazlitt: A Record of Personal Relationship and Critical Estimate." *PMLA* 62 (June 1947):487–502.

_____. *The Mind of John Keats.* New York: Oxford University Press, 1926.

Vogler, Thomas A. *Preludes to Vision: The Epic Venture in Blake, Wordsworth, Keats, and Hart Crane.* Berkeley and Los Angeles: University of California Press, 1971.

Wagner, Robert D. "Keats: 'Ode to Psyche' and the Second 'Hyperion.' " *Keats-Shelley Journal* 13 (Winter 1964):29–41.

Ward, Aileen. *John Keats.* New York: Viking Press, 1963.

Warton, Joseph. *An Essay on The Genius and Writings of Pope.* 2 vols. 5th ed. London, 1806.

Warton, Thomas. *Observations on the Fairy Queen of Spenser.* 2 vols. London: Printed by C. Stower, 1807.

Wasserman, Earl R. *The Finer Tone: Keats' Major Poems.* Baltimore: Johns Hopkins Press, 1967.

_____. *Shelley's Prometheus Unbound.* Baltimore: Johns Hopkins Press, 1965.

_____. *The Subtler Language: Critical Readings of Neoclassic and Romantic Poems.* Baltimore: Johns Hopkins Press, 1959.

Weller, Earle V., ed. *Keats and Mary Tighe.* New York: Century Co., for Modern Language Association of America, 1928.

West, Paul, ed. *Byron: A Collection of Critical Essays.* Englewood Cliffs, N.J.: Prentice-Hall, 1963.

Wigod, Jacob D. "The Meaning of *Endymion.*" *PMLA* 68 (1953):779–90.

Wilkie, Brian. *Romantic Poets and Epic Tradition.* Madison and Milwaukee: University of Wisconsin Press, 1965.

Woolf, Virginia. *A Writer's Diary.* Edited by Leonard Woolf. London: Hogarth Press, 1954.

Acknowledgments

I wish to thank the Office of Research and Projects of the Graduate School, Southern Illinois University, for research funds which enabled me to complete this book. I am also grateful to Professors James Benziger and George Goodin, of Southern Illinois University, who read parts of the book at various stages. My special thanks goes to Professor Bernice Slote of the University of Nebraska–Lincoln for the careful attention which she gave to the manuscript.

J.L.

Index

Index